D1058003

A Short Method of Prayer & Other Writings

A SHORT METHOD OF PRAYER

&

OTHER WRITINGS

MADAME GUYON

HENDRICKSON
Christian
Classics

A Short Method of Prayer and Other Writings

© 2005 by Hendrickson Publishers, Inc.

Hendrickson Publishers, Inc.
P. O. Box 3473
Peabody, Massachusetts 01961–3473

ISBN: 1-56563-941-3

Printed in the United States of America

First Printing—September 2005

A Short and Easy Method of Prayer was originally published in French in 1685 as *Moyen court et tres facile pour l'oraison* (A short and very easy method of prayer). The English text used in this edition was published in London in 1907.

Spiritual Torrents (Les torrents spirituels) was written in French in 1682. The English translation used in this edition was published in London in 1908.

Contents

Preface

Hendrickson Christian Classics Edition

Madam Jeanne Marie Bouvier de la Mothe Guyon
(1648–1717)

Maybe John Wesley was right when he proffered that Christianity might "search many centuries to find another woman who was such a pattern of true holiness" as Madame Jeanne Marie de la Mothe Guyon. They weren't quite contemporaries; in 1703, when Wesley was born, she was fifty-five and banished to Blois, a small city in central France, her health broken by a four-year imprisonment in the Bastille. But Wesley clearly knew of her reputation and writings on the sanctified life—a theme he preached and expounded.

As a Roman Catholic laywoman, Madame Guyon never preached formal sermons; she didn't address large crowds, and yet her classic biographer, Thomas Upham,[1] piercingly summarized her spiritual influence, which unwittingly spilled into the world of politics:

> It is remarkable, that a man [Louis XIV] whose mind was occupied with plans of vast extent, such as perhaps no French monarch before him had entertained, should enter into a contest, which may well be called a personal contest, with an unprotected woman. But so it was.

Jeanne Marie de la Mothe was born in 1648 to a noteworthy noble family fifty miles south of Paris. Pampered and encouraged by her pious father, she was trained and taught in various local convents, voraciously reading and memorizing Scripture. Beautiful, intelligent, articulate . . . at sixteen she entered into an arranged marriage with a man twenty years older than she—a marriage made hellish not so much by the husband as by his ever-present mother. "My proud spirit broke under her system of coercion. . . . I found myself a slave in my own dwelling."

The twelve years of her marriage brought other hardships, including disfiguring small pox and the death of two young children, but also graces and growth. At age twenty, she sought advice from a Franciscan, who listened to her complaints of spiritual dryness and whose response prompted her spiritual awakening:

> Your efforts have been unsuccessful, Madame, because you have sought without, what you can only find within. Accustom yourself to seek God in your heart, and you will not fail to find him.

She describes the experience.

> I felt at this instant deeply wounded with the love of God—a wound so delightful, that I desired it never might be healed.

Prompted by this love, she felt compelled to set a new course, engaging in extensive charitable work, generously dispensing discretionary financial resources to the poor, tending the sick, and providing trade-training to vulnerable girls, even as she tended to her family. Ever more deeply committed to God, she met and informally introduced a vibrant spirituality to a priest who would be her compatriot for years to come, Francis de la Combe.

---

[1] T. C. Upham: *The Life of Madame Guyon*; Allenson & Co., London, 1905.

For several years before and after her husband's death in 1676, Jeanne suffered a spiritual depression, which permanently lifted after a day of intense prayer. Biographer Upham noted:

> She was led for the first time to see, under the intimations of the Holy Spirit, that all things were just the reverse of what she had supposed—that affliction is mercy in disguise, that we possess by first being deprived, that death precedes life, that destruction in the spiritual experience turns to renovation, that out of the sorrows and silence of inward crucifixion, and from no other source, must grow the jubilees of everlasting bliss.

In her posthumously published *Autobiography*, she wrote,

> What I had possessed some years before, in the period of my spiritual enjoyment, was consolation, peace—the *gift* of God rather than the Giver; but now, I was brought into such harmony with the will of God, that I might now be said to possess not merely consolation, but *the God* of consolation; not merely peace, but *the God* of peace.

In this sanctifying experience, by faith she aligned her will with God's, as she would later describe in her book *Spiritual Torrents.*

After putting her husband's estate in order, seeking ecclesiastical clearance, and making provision for the care and education of two sons, Jeanne, now aged thirty-four, left France to engage in not-well-defined charitable missionary work near Geneva. Her life would never be the same, as prophetically suggested in a scene played out as her party of five—a female companion, two maids, and her own young daughter—left Paris. In a boat, on the Seine, the five-year-old girl amused herself with twigs and reeds, tearing and folding them into numerous crosses, which she then attached to her mother's clothing. When another traveler requested, "Give me some crosses too," the girl replied, "No, they are all for my mother." Continuing her play, the girl uncannily wove a crown of leaves and placed it on her mother's head, announcing, "After the cross you shall be crowned."

Once in the shadow of the Alps, Jeanne set her hand to "making ointments," tending the sick, even founding a hospital. But with increasing urgency, she felt God had brought her here for yet another purpose—to expound her understanding of sanctification by faith. This went beyond justification or forgiveness by faith. It had no relation to attempted sanctification by self-will or self-mortification. It was sanctification or holiness by faith, as one renounced self and as one's will became one with God's will. One didn't possess simply God's gifts; one possessed the Giver. As Paul wrote, "I live; and yet not I, but Christ liveth in me."

Joined by her spiritual director, Francis de la Combe (who was directing whom?) Jeanne became an influential presence. Upham asserted that the local bishop

> had the sagacity to perceive, that the responsibility for this movement, which both excited his curiosity and alarmed his fears, rested chiefly upon Madame Guyon,

though La Combe was preaching the sermons. The bishop "had approved of her coming" to the diocese "as an executor of charities, and not as a teacher of dogmatics."

Church-instigated harassment—if not persecution—heated up, her window sashes broken, her mail intercepted . . . causing her to move from one city to another, where her upstanding and credible reputation spread among the laity.

Ultimately, in 1684, the bishop who had invited her to his diocese demanded that she leave—but not before she had written the first of her manuscripts, *Spiritual Torrents*, which she called a "treatise on the principle of Faith, considered in its inward and sanctifying action." The title is suggested by Amos 5:24: Let righteousness roll down as a mighty torrent. The text compares the spiritual progress of the soul to a stream or river descending from the mountains to the huge ocean, representing the holy God. This early work is strongly influenced by, and descriptive of, the progression of her own spiritual journey. It is a highly imaginative work, the metaphor sometimes running away with itself.

When she settled in Grenoble, Jeanne's following grew. She notes,

> People flocked together from all sides, far and near. Friars, priests, men of the world, maids, wives, widows, all came, one after another, to hear what was to be said. So great was the interest felt, that for some time I was wholly occupied from six o'clock in the morning till eight in the evening, in speaking of God.

Yet at night she found time to work on what would eventually be an "experimental and practical" Bible commentary, working not from Hebrew and Greek, but from Latin, French, and Italian sources.

Commenting on her large local audience, her *Autobiography* mentioned several clerics who were "grievously chagrined that a woman should be so much flocked to and sought after." Yet she won them over, and wrote *A Short and Easy Method of Prayer* to address, in part, needs she noted in the novices under their care. The text does not discount the role of rote prayers, including the Lord's Prayer; but saying and slowly pondering the "Our Father" is only the "first degree" of prayer, followed by contemplation and silence, communing with the Holy Spirit within.

The manuscript wasn't meant for broad distribution, but was published in 1685 by a friend who was a "counselor of the Parliament of Grenoble." Its content was so controversial and such a threat to many—not all—in the Catholic Church that she fled Grenoble on the advice of supporters, including the local bishop.

This "new spirituality"—similar to that deemed heretical in a contemporary Italian Jesuit, Michael de Molinos—became known as Quietism, a movement within the Catholic Church that talked so much about faith and spiritual renewal that it "smelled" like Protestantism. But it included a spiritual emptying of self and surrender to Providence that rendered one passive in a worldly sense, though not without duty prompted by Pure Love. Molinos wrote:

> If thou receivest an injury from any man, remember that there are two things in it, viz., the sin of him who does it, and the suffering which is inflicted on thyself. The sin is against the will of God, and it greatly displeases him though he permits it. But the suffering which thou art called to endure, is not in opposition to his will. But, on the contrary, he wills it for thy good. Wherefore, thou oughtest to receive it as from his hand.

In July 1686 Jeanne settled back in Paris, where she was, for a while, welcomed by countesses and duchesses—her ministry reaching into the royal courts. But opposition prevailed. In October 1687 Louis XIV sent La Combe to the Bastille, where he was confined until the year of his death, 1714. Subsequently, when accusers brought to the king a forged letter in which Madame Guyon purportedly said she had "great designs in hand" to hold religious meetings around Paris, Louis confined (imprisoned) her in an austere convent for eight months. The threat? Upham noted: "he saw the germs of another Protestantism springing up in his own city and under his own eye."

Upham also provided this commentary of her theological stance as it relates to her imprisonment:

> The doctrines of Sanctification, to which she was so much attached, involved principles peculiarly adapted to such a situation. . . . They annihilate times and places, prosperities and adversities, friendships and enmities, by making them all equal in the will of God. So that to Joseph the prison and the throne are the same, to Daniel the lion's den and the monarch's palace are the same, because they have that in their believing and sanctified hearts, which subjects the outward to the inward, and because the inward has become incorporated by faith in that Eternal Will in which all things have their origin and their end.

In the course of this imprisonment, she gave a formidable defense of her views before an ecclesiastical judge and might have been set free—if she had consented to the betrothal of her twelve-year-old daughter to a dissolute marquis. Her response? "I can never buy my liberty at the expense of sacrificing my daughter." Her biographer continued: "After this, things looked more unfavorably."

Through the royal intercession of a courtly woman, Louis did release Guyon, and her ecclesiastical cause was picked up by the Abbé de Fénelon, a priest of noble birth and soon-to-be archbishop of Cambrai, who at this point was in good standing with the king. His nemesis was Bossuet, bishop of Meaux, "confessedly the leader of the French Church." Again called to defend her "new spirituality" as it was called, Jeanne wrote *A Concise Apology for the Short and Easy Method of Prayer,* and held her own in extensive interviews with Bossuet.

After eight years of freedom, she was arrested in 1695 and imprisoned at the castle of Vincennes and then the famed Bastille till 1702. Her health broken, Jeanne was released at age fifty-four and banished to Blois, a hundred miles southwest of Paris. "The extreme deprivations and trials of the Bastille had effectually broken a constitution but feeble before," wrote her biographer.

Until her death in 1717, her physical world was small, and yet her influence remained.

> Great numbers of persons came to see her. . . . Forgetful of herself, she regulated her remarks exclusively by a regard to the spiritual state and the wants of those who thus had interviews with her.

In these years she finished the autobiographical tome she had started years before, during her first imprisonment. When friends pressed her to publish it, she consented, with the stipulation that it be printed posthumously.

Though she steadfastly claimed loyalty to the Catholic Church, Madame Guyon's greatest historical influence—themes of holiness and submission to Providence—has been in Protestant circles, especially in England and Holland.

> *We should forget ourselves, and all self-interest, and listen and be attentive to the voice of our God; and these two simple actions, or rather passive dispositions, attract his love to that beauty which he himself communicates.*

—M. Guyon, *A Short and Easy Method of Prayer*

A Short and Easy
Method of Prayer

PREFACE

TO THE 1907 ALLENSON EDITION

This little book has exercised a very great influence in both secular and religious circles. It was published at the suggestion of a friend. Madame Guyon thus speaks of it:[1]

> Among my intimate friends was a civilian, a counselor of the Parliament of Grenoble, who might be described as a model of piety. Seeing on my table my manuscript treatise on Prayer, he desired me to lend it to him. Being much pleased with it, he lent it to some of his friends. Others wanted copies of it. He resolved, therefore, to have it printed. I was requested to write a preface, which I did.

It immediately won a great notoriety, five or six editions being required in a very short time. It became the storm-center in France for a number of years, and was directly the cause of Madame Guyon being attacked and defended by some of the most brilliant writers of her day. Bossuet opposed, and Fénelon as vigorously, and ultimately with complete success, supported the

---

[1] T. C. Upham: *The Life of Madame Guyon*; Allenson & Co., London, 1905, p. 234.

3

gentle authoress. In the meantime the result upon Madame Guyon was imprisonment in the Bastille!

It has, too, had weighty effect upon English history, particularly in its influence upon the school of modern Christian Mysticism.

The reader is advised that the versions of the Bible to which Madame Guyon in 1685 had opportunity of access were not the same as theirs of today, and therefore oftentimes discrepancies apparently occur in her quotations from the Bible. Very often, too, she is quoting direct from the Vulgate.

The Author's Preface

to the Original Edition

This little treatise, conceived in great simplicity, was not originally intended for publication: it was written for a few individuals, who were desirous to love God with their whole heart; some of whom, because of the profit they received in reading the manuscript, wished to obtain copies of it; and on this account alone, it was committed to the press.

It still remains in its original simplicity, without any censure on the various divine leadings of others: and we submit the whole to the judgment of those who are skilled and experienced in divine matters; requesting them, however, not to decide without first entering into the main design of the Author, which is to induce the world to love God and to serve him with comfort and success, in a simple and easy manner, adapted to those who are unqualified for learned and deep researches, and are, indeed, incapable of anything but a hearty desire to be truly devoted to God.

An unprejudiced reader may find hidden under the most common expressions, a secret unction, which will excite him to seek after that Sovereign Good, whom all should wish to enjoy.

In speaking of the attainment of perfection, the word *Facility* is used, because God is indeed found with facility when we seek him within ourselves. But, in contradiction to this, some perhaps may urge that passage in John, "Ye shall seek me, and shall not find me" (John 7:34). This apparent difficulty, however, is removed by another passage, where he, who cannot contradict himself, hath said to all, "Seek and ye shall find" (Matt. 7:7). It is true, indeed, that he who would seek God, and is yet unwilling to forsake his sins, shall not find him, because he seeks not aright; and therefore it is added, "Ye shall die in your sins." On the other hand, he who diligently seeks God in his heart, and that he may draw near unto him sincerely forsakes sin, shall infallibly find him.

A life of devotion appears so formidable, and the Spirit of Prayer of such difficult attainment, that most persons are discouraged from taking a single step towards it. The difficulties inseparable from all great undertakings are, indeed, either nobly surmounted, or left to subsist in all their terrors, just as success is the object of despair or hope. I have therefore endeavored to show the facility of the method proposed in this treatise, the great advantages to be derived from it, and the certainty of their attainment by those that faithfully persevere.

O! were we once truly sensible of the goodness of God toward his poor creatures, and of his infinite desire to communicate himself unto them, we should not allow imaginary difficulties to affright us, nor despair of obtaining that good which he is so earnest to bestow: "He that spared not his own son, but delivered him up for us all; how shall he not, with him, also freely give us all things?" (Rom. 8:32). But we want courage and perseverance; we have both to a high degree in our temporal concerns, but want them in "the one thing needful" (Luke 10:42).

If any think that God is not easily to be found in this way of Simple Love and Pure Adherence, let them not, on my testimony, alter their opinion, but rather make trial of it, and their own experience will convince them that the reality far exceeds all my representations of it.

Beloved reader, peruse this little treatise with a humble, sincere and candid spirit, and not with an inclination to cavil and criticize, and you will not fail to reap some degree of profit from it. It was written with a hearty desire that you might wholly devote yourself to God; receive it, then, with a like desire for your own perfection: for nothing more is intended by it than to invite the simple and child-like to approach their Father, who delights in the humble confidence of his children, and is grieved at the smallest instance of their diffidence or distrust. With a sincere desire, therefore, to forsake sin, seek nothing from the unpretending method here proposed but the Love of God, and you shall undoubtedly obtain it.

Without setting up our opinions above those of others, we mean only, with truth and candor, to declare, from our own experience and the experience of others, the happy effects produced by thus simply following our Lord.

As this treatise was intended only to instruct in Prayer, there are many things which we respect and esteem, totally omitted, as not immediately relative to our main subject: it is, however, certain, that nothing will be found herein to offend, provided it be read in the spirit with which it was written; and it is still more certain, that those who in right earnest make trial of the way, will find we have written the Truth.

It is thou alone, O holy Jesus, who lovest simplicity and innocence, "and whose delight is to dwell with the children of men" (Prov. 8:3), with those who are, indeed, willing to become "little children"; it is thou alone, who canst render this little work of any value by imprinting it on the hearts of all who read it, and leading them to seek thee within themselves, where thou reposest as in the manger, waiting to receive proofs of their love, and to give them testimony of thine. Yet alas! They may still lose these unspeakable advantages by their negligence and insensibility! But it belongeth unto thee, O thou Uncreated Love! Thou Silent and Eternal Word! it belongeth unto thee, to awaken, attract, and convert; to make thyself be heard, tasted, and beloved! I know thou canst do it, and I trust thou wilt do it by this humble work which belongeth entirely to Thee, proceedeth wholly from thee, and tendeth only to thee! And, O most gracious and adorable Savior—to thee be all the glory!

CHAPTER I

The Universal Call to Prayer

What a dreadful delusion hath prevailed over the greater part of mankind, in supposing that they are not called to a state of prayer! Whereas all are capable of prayer, and are called thereto, as all are called to and are capable of salvation.

Prayer is the application of the heart to God, and the internal exercise of love. S. Paul hath enjoined us to "pray without ceasing" (1 Thess. 5:17), and our Lord saith, "I say unto you all, watch and pray" (Mark 13:33, 37): all therefore *may*, and all *ought* to practice prayer. I grant that meditation is attainable but by few, for few are capable of it; and therefore, my beloved brethren who are athirst for salvation, meditative prayer is not the prayer which God requires of you, nor which we would recommend.

Let all pray: we should live by prayer, as we should live by love. "I counsel you to buy of me gold tried in the fire, that ye may be rich" (Rev. 3:8)—this is much more easily obtained than we can conceive. "Come, all ye that are athirst, to these living waters"; nor lose your precious moments in "hewing out cisterns, broken cisterns that will hold no water" (John

8

7:37; Jer 2:13). Come, ye famished souls, who find naught whereon to feed; come, and ye shall be fully satisfied!

Come, ye poor afflicted ones, who groan beneath your load of wretchedness and pain, and ye shall find ease and comfort! Come, ye sick, to your Physician, and be not fearful of approaching him because ye are filled with diseases; expose them to his view and they shall be healed!

Children, draw near to your Father, and he will embrace you in the arms of love! Come, ye poor, stray, wandering sheep, return to your Shepherd! Come, sinners, to your Savior! Come, ye dull, ignorant, and illiterate, ye who think yourselves the most incapable of prayer! Ye are more peculiarly called and adapted thereto. Let all without exception come, for Jesus Christ hath called all.

Yet let not those come who are without a heart; they are not asked; for there must be a heart, that there may be love. But who is without a heart? O come, then, give this heart to God; and here learn how to make the donation.

All who are desirous of prayer may easily pray, enabled by those ordinary graces and gifts of the Holy Spirit which are common to all men.

Prayer is the guide to perfection and the sovereign good; it delivers us from every vice, and obtains us every virtue; for the one great means to become perfect, is to walk in the presence of God: he himself hath said, "walk in my presence and be ye perfect" (Gen. 17:1). It is by prayer alone that we are brought into this presence, and maintained in it without interruption.

You must then learn a species of prayer, which may be exercised at all times; which doth not obstruct outward employments; and which may be equally practiced by princes, kings, prelates, priests and magistrates, soldiers and children, tradesmen, laborers, women and sick persons: it cannot, therefore, be the prayer of the head, but of the heart; not a prayer of the understanding alone, which is so limited in its operations that it can have but one object at one time; but the prayer of the heart is not interrupted by the exercises of reason: indeed nothing can interrupt this prayer, but irregular and disordered affections: and when once we have tasted of God, and the sweetness of his love, we shall find it impossible to relish aught but himself?

Nothing is so easily obtained as the possession and enjoyment of God, for "in him we live, move, and have our being;" and he is more desirous to give himself into us, than we can be to receive him.

All consists in the manner of seeking him; and to seek aright, is easier and more natural to us than breathing. Though you think yourselves ever so stupid, dull, and incapable of sublime attainments, yet, by prayer, you may live in God himself with less difficulty or interruption than you live in the vital air. Will it not then be highly sinful to neglect prayer? But this I trust you will not, when you have learnt the method, which is exceedingly easy.

Chapter 2

The Method of Prayer

There are two ways of introducing a soul into prayer, which should for some time be pursued; the one is Meditation, the other is Reading accompanied with Meditation.

Meditative Reading is the choosing some important practical or speculative truth, always preferring the practical, and proceeding thus: whatever truth you have chosen, read only a small portion of it, endeavoring to taste and digest it, to extract the essence and substance thereof, and proceed no farther while any savor or relish remains in the passage: when this subsides, take up your book again and proceed as before, seldom reading more than half a page at a time, for it is not the quantity that is read, but the manner of reading, that yields us profit.

Those who read fast reap no more advantage than a bee would by only skimming over the surface of the flower, instead of waiting to penetrate into it, and extract its sweets. Much reading is rather for scholastic subjects than divine truths: indeed, to receive real profit from spiritual books, we must read as I have described; and I am certain, if that method were pursued, we should become gradually habituated to, and more fully disposed for prayer.

Meditation, which is the other method, is to be practiced at an appropriated season, and not in the time of reading. I believe the best manner of meditating is as follows: when, by an act of lively faith, you are placed in the Presence of God, recollect some truth wherein there is substance and food; pause gently and sweetly thereon, not to employ the reason, but merely to calm and fix the mind: for you must observe, that your principal exercise should ever be the Presence of God; your subject, therefore, should rather serve to stay the mind, than exercise the understanding.

From this procedure, it will necessarily follow, that the lively faith in a God immediately present in our inmost soul, will produce an eager and vehement pressing inwardly into ourselves, and a restraining all our senses from wandering abroad: this serves to extricate us speedily from numberless distractions, to remove us far from external objects, and to bring us nigh unto our God, who is only to be found in our inmost center, which is the Holy of Holies wherein he dwelleth.

He hath even promised "to come and make his abode with him that doth his will" (John 14:23). S. Augustine accuses himself of wasting his time, by not having from the first, sought God in this manner of prayer.

When we are thus fully introverted, and warmly penetrated throughout with a living sense of the Divine Presence; when the senses are all recollected, and withdrawn from the circumference to the center, and the soul is sweetly and silently employed on the truths we have read, not in reasoning, but in feeding thereon, and in animating the will by affection, rather than fatiguing the understanding by study; when, I say, the affections are in this state (which, however difficult it may appear at first, is, as I shall hereafter show, easily attainable); we must allow them sweetly to repose, and peacefully to drink in that of which they have tasted. For as a person may enjoy the flavor of the finest viand in mastication, yet receive no nourishment therefrom, if he does not cease the action and swallow the food; so, when our affections are enkindled, if we endeavor to stir them up yet more, we extinguish their flame, and the soul is deprived of its nourishment. We should, therefore, in stillness and repose, with respect, confidence and love, swallow the blessed food of which we have tasted. This method is, indeed, highly necessary, and will advance the soul farther in a short time, than any other in a course of years.

I have mentioned that our direct and principal exercise should consist in the contemplation of the Divine Presence: we should be also exceedingly watchful and diligent in recalling our dissipated senses, as the most easy method of overcoming distractions; for a direct contest and opposition only serves to irritate and augment them. Whereas, by sinking down under a sense and perception of a present God, and by simply turning inwards, we wage insensibly a very advantageous, though indirect war with them.

It is proper here to caution beginners against wandering from truth to truth, and from subject to subject: the right way to penetrate every divine truth, to enjoy its full relish, and to imprint it on the heart, is dwelling on it whilst its savor continues.

Though recollection is difficult in the beginning, from the habit the soul has acquired of being always from home; yet, when by the violence it hath done itself, it becometh a little accustomed to it, it will soon be rendered perfectly easy, and become delightful. Such is the experimental taste and sense of his Presence, and such the efficacy of those graces, which that God bestows, whose One Will towards his creatures is to communicate himself unto them!

CHAPTER 3

The First Degree of Prayer

Those who have not learnt to read, are not, on that account, excluded from prayer; for the Great Book which teacheth all things, and which is legible as well internally as externally, is Jesus Christ himself.

The method they should practice is this: they should first learn this fundamental truth, that "the kingdom of God is within them" (Luke 17:21), and that it is there, only it must be sought.

It is as incumbent on the clergy to instruct their parishioners in prayer, as in their catechism. It is true, they tell them the end [objective] of their creation; but should they not also give them sufficient instructions how they may attain it? They should be taught to begin by an act of profound adoration and abasement before God; and closing the corporeal eyes, endeavor to open those of the soul: they should then collect themselves inwardly, and, by a lively faith in God, as dwelling within them, pierce into the Divine Presence; not suffering the senses to wander abroad, but withholding them as much as may be in due subjection.

They should then repeat the Lord's Prayer in their native tongue, pondering a little upon the meaning of the words, and the infinite willingness of that God who dwells within them, to become, indeed, their Father. In this state let them pour out their wants before him; and when they have pronounced the endearing word, "Father," remain a few moments in a respectful silence, waiting to have the will of this, their heavenly Father, made manifest unto them.

Again, beholding themselves in the state of a feeble child, sorely bruised by repeated falls, and defiled in the mire, destitute of strength to keep up, or of power to cleanse himself, they should lay their deplorable situation open to their Father's view in humble confusion; now sighing out a few words of love and plaintive sorrow, and again sinking into profound silence before him. Then, continuing the Lord's Prayer, let them beseech this King of Glory to reign in them, yielding to his love the just claim he has over them, and resigning up themselves wholly to his divine government.

If they feel an inclination to peace and silence, let them discontinue the words of the prayer so long as this sensation holds; and when it subsides, go on with the second petition, "Thy will be done on earth, as it is in heaven!" upon which these humble supplicants must beseech God to accomplish, in them, and by them, all his will; and must surrender their hearts and freedom into his hands, to be disposed of as he pleaseth. And finding that the best employment of the will is to love, they should desire to love God with all their strength, and implore him for his pure love; but all this sweetly and peacefully: and so of the rest of the prayer, in which the clergy may instruct them. But they should not overburden themselves with frequent repetitions of set forms or studied prayers (Matt. 6:7); for the Lord's Prayer, once repeated as I have just described, will produce abundant fruit.

At other times they should place themselves as sheep before their Shepherd, looking up to him for their true substantial food: "O Divine Shepherd, thou feedest thy flock with thyself, and art, indeed, their daily nourishment!" They may also represent unto him the necessities of their families: but all upon this principle, and in this one great view of faith, that God is within them.

The ideas we form of the Divine Being fall infinitely short of what he is: a lively *faith* in his presence is sufficient: for we must not form any image of the Deity; though we may of the Second Person in the ever-blessed Trinity, beholding him in the various states of his Incarnation, from his birth to his crucifixion, or in some other state or mystery, provided the soul always seeks for those views in its inmost ground or center.

Again, we may look to him as our Physician, and present to his healing influence all our maladies; but always without violence or perturbation, and from time to time with pauses of silence, that being intermingled with the action, the silence may be gradually extended, and our own exertion lessened; till at length, by continually yielding to God's operations, they gain the complete ascendancy; as shall be hereafter explained.

When the Divine Presence is granted us, and we gradually relish silence and repose, this experimental feeling and taste of the Presence of God introduces the soul into the second degree of prayer, which, by proceeding in the manner I have described, is attainable as well by the illiterate as the learned. Some favored souls, indeed, are indulged with it, even from the beginning.

CHAPTER 4

The Second Degree of Prayer

Some call the second degree of prayer, "The Prayer of Contemplation," or "The Prayer of Faith and Stillness," and others call it, "The Prayer of Simplicity." I shall here use this latter appellation, as being more just than any of the former, which imply a much more exalted state of prayer than that I am now treating of.

When the soul has been for some time exercised in the way I have mentioned, it finds that it is gradually enabled to approach God with facility; that recollection is attended with much less difficulty; and that prayer becomes easy, sweet, and delightful. It knows that this is the true way of finding God; and feels "his name is as ointment poured forth" (Cant. 1-3). But the method must now be altered, and that which I prescribe, [be] followed with courage and fidelity, without being disturbed at the difficulties we may encounter therein.

First [most importantly], as soon as the soul by faith places itself in the Presence of God, and becomes recollected before him, let it remain thus for a little time in a profound and respectful silence.

But if, at the beginning, in forming the act of faith, it feels some little pleasing sense of the Divine Presence; let it remain there without being troubled for a subject, and proceed no farther, but carefully cherish this sensation while it continues: as soon as it abates, the will may be excited by some tender affection; and if by the first moving thereof, it finds itself reinstated in sweet peace, let it there remain: the smothered fire must be gently fanned; but as soon as it is kindled, we must cease that effort, lest we extinguish it by our own activity.

I would warmly recommend it to all, never to finish prayer without remaining some little time after in a respectful silence. It is also of the greatest importance for the soul to go to prayer with courage, and such a pure and disinterested love, as seeks nothing from God, but the ability to please him, and to do his will: for a servant who only proportions his diligence to his hope of reward, renders himself unworthy of all reward.

Go then to prayer, not that ye may enjoy spiritual delights, but that ye may be either full or empty, just as it pleaseth God: this will preserve you in an evenness of spirit, in desertion as well as in consolation, and prevent your being surprised at aridity or the apparent repulses of God.

CHAPTER 5

Of Spiritual Aridity

Though God hath no other desire than to impart himself to the loving soul that seeks him, yet he frequently conceals himself that the soul may be roused from sloth, and impelled to seek him with fidelity and love. But with what abundant goodness doth he recompense the faithfulness of his beloved? And how sweetly are these apparent withdrawings of himself succeeded by the consoling caresses of love?

At these seasons we are apt to believe, either that it proves our fidelity, and evinces a greater ardor of affection, to seek him by an exertion of our own strength and activity; or, that this exertion will induce him the more speedily to revisit us.

No, no, my dear souls, believe me, this is not the right procedure in this degree of prayer. With patient love, with self-abasement and humiliation, with the reiterated breathings of an ardent but peaceful affection, and with silence full of the most profound respect, you must wait the return of the Beloved. Thus only you will demonstrate that it is himself alone, and his good pleasure, that you seek; and not the selfish delights of your own sensations. Hence it is said,

> Be not impatient in the time of dryness and obscurity; suffer the sus-
> pension and delays of the consolations of God; cleave unto him, and
> wait upon him, patiently, that thy life may increase and be renewed.
> (Eccles. 2:2–3)

Be ye, therefore, patient in prayer, though, during life, you can do naught else than wait the return of the Beloved, in deep humiliation, calm contentment, and patient resignation to his will. And yet how this most excellent prayer may be intermingled with the sighings of plaintive love! This conduct, indeed, is most pleasing to the heart of Jesus; and, above all others, will, as it were, compel him to return.

CHAPTER 6

Of Self-Surrender

We should now begin to abandon and give up our whole existence unto God, from the strong and positive conviction, that the occurrence of every moment is agreeable to his immediate will and permission, and just such as our state requires. This conviction will make us resigned in all things; and accept of all that happens, not as from the creature, but as from God himself.

But I conjure you, my dearly beloved, who sincerely wish to give up yourselves to God, that after you have made the donation, you will not snatch yourselves back again. Remember: a gift once presented is no longer at the disposal of the donor.

Abandonment is a matter of the greatest importance in our process; it is the key to the inner court; so that whosoever knoweth truly how to abandon himself, soon becomes perfect: we must, therefore, continue steadfast and immovable therein, nor listen to the voice of natural reason. Great faith produces great abandonment: we must confide in God "hoping against hope" (Rom. 4:18).

Abandonment is the casting off of all selfish care, that we may be altogether at the Divine Disposal. All Christians are exhorted to this resignation: for it is said to all, "Be not anxious for tomorrow, for your heavenly Father knoweth all that is necessary for you" (Matt. 20:25). "In all thy ways acknowledge him, and he shall direct thy paths" (Prov. 3:6). "Commit thy ways unto the Lord, and thy thoughts shall be established" (Prov. 16:3). "Commit thy ways unto the Lord, and he himself will bring it to pass" (Psa. 36:5).

Our abandonment then should be as fully applied to external as internal things, giving up all our concerns into the hands of God, forgetting ourselves, and thinking only of him; by which the heart will remain always disengaged, free, and at peace. It is practiced by continually losing our own will in the will of God; by renouncing every particular inclination as soon as it arises, however good it may appear, that we may stand in indifference with respect to ourselves, and only will that which God from eternity hath willed; by being resigned in all things, whether for soul or body, whether for time or eternity; by leaving what is past in oblivion, what is to come to Providence, and devoting the present moment to God, which brings with itself God's eternal order, and is as infallible a declaration to us of his will as it is inevitable and common to all; by attributing nothing that befalls us to the creature, but regarding all things in God, and looking upon all, excepting only our sins, as infallibly proceeding from him. Surrender yourselves, then, to be led and disposed of just as God pleaseth, with respect both to your outward and inward state.

CHAPTER 7

Of Sufferings

Be patient under all the sufferings which God is pleased to send you: if your love to him be pure, you will not seek him less on Calvary, than on Tabor;[1] and, surely, he should be as much loved on that as on this, since it was on Calvary he made the greater display of his Love for you.

Be not like those, who give themselves to him at one season, and withdraw from him at another: they give themselves only to be caressed; and wrest themselves back again, when they come to be crucified, or at least turn for consolation to the creature.

No, beloved souls, ye will not find consolation in aught, but in the love of the cross, and in total abandonment: "Whosoever favoreth not the

---

[1] Mount Tabor in Israel is mentioned more than half a dozen times in the King James Bible. At Tabor, Israel surrounded and destroyed the Canaanite army led by Sisera, recorded in Judges 4-5. "Then Deborah said to Barak, 'Go! This is the day the Lord has given Sisera into your hands. Has not the Lord gone ahead of you?' So Barak went down Mount Tabor, followed by ten thousand men." (v. 4:14, emphasis added.) Another reference is in Jeremiah 46, where God warns the Israelites that "Nebuchadrezzar, king of Babylon, should come and smite the land of Egypt." (v. 13) God says, "As I live, saith the King, whose name is the Lord of hosts, *Surely as Tabor is among the mountains,* and as Carmel by the sea, so shall he come." (v. 18, emphasis added.)

cross, favoreth not the things that be of God" (Matt. 16:23). It is impossible to love God without loving the cross; and a heart that favors the cross, finds the bitterest things to be sweet. "A famished soul findeth bitter things sweet" (Job. 6:1) because it findeth itself hungering for God, in proportion as it hungereth for the cross. God giveth the cross, and the cross giveth us God.

We may be assured that there is an internal advancement, where there is an advancement in the way of the cross: abandonment and the cross go hand in hand together.

As soon as suffering presents itself, and you feel a repugnance against it, resign yourself immediately unto God with respect to it, and give yourself up to him in sacrifice; you shall find, that, when the cross arrives, it will not be so very burdensome, because you had disposed yourself to a willing reception of it. This, however, does not prevent your feeling its weight as some have imagined; for when we do not feel the cross, we do not suffer it. A sensibility of sufferings constitutes a principal part of the sufferings themselves. Jesus Christ himself was willing to suffer its utmost rigors. We often bear the cross in weakness, at other times in strength; all should be equal to us in the will of God.

CHAPTER 8

Of Mysteries

It may be objected, that, by this method, we shall have no mysteries imprinted on our minds: but it is quite the reverse; for it is the peculiar means of imparting them to the soul. Jesus Christ, to whom we are abandoned, and whom "we follow as the way, whom we hear as the truth, and who animates us as the life" (John 14:6), in imprinting himself on the soul, impresses the characters of his different states; and to bear all the states of Jesus Christ is far more sublime, than merely to reason concerning them. S. Paul bore in his body the states of Jesus Christ: "I bear in my body," says he, "the marks of the Lord Jesus" (Gal. 6:17), but he does not say that he reasoned [understood] thereon.

In our acts of resignation, Jesus Christ frequently communicates some peculiar views or revelations of his states: these we should thankfully receive, and dispose ourselves for what appeareth to be his will. Indeed, having no other choice, but that of ardently reaching after him, of dwelling ever with him, and of sinking into nothingness before him, we should accept indiscriminately all his dispensations, whether obscurity or illumination, fruitfulness or barrenness, weakness or strength, sweetness or bitterness, temptations, distractions, pain, weariness, or doubtings; and none of all these should, for one moment, retard our course.

God engages some, for whole years, in the contemplation and enjoyment of a particular mystery; the simple view or contemplation of which gathers the soul inward, provided it be faithful: but as soon as God is pleased to withdraw this view from the soul, it should freely yield to the deprivation. Some are very uneasy at feeling their inability to meditate on certain mysteries; but this disquietude hath no just foundation, since an affectionate attachment to God includes every species of devotion: for whosoever, in repose and quiet, is united to God alone, is, indeed, most excellently and effectually applied to every divine mystery: the Love of God comprehends, in itself, the love of all that appertains to him.

CHAPTER 9

Of Virtue

It is thus we acquire virtue, with facility and certainty; for, as God is the fountain and principle of all virtue, we possess all in the possession of him; and in proportion as we approach toward this possession, in like proportion do we rise into the most eminent virtues. For all virtue is but as a mask, an outside appearance changeable as our garments, if it doth not spring up, and issue from within; and then, indeed, it is genuine, essential, and permanent: "The beauty of the King's daughter proceeds from within" saith David (Psa. 45:14). These souls, above all others, practice virtue in the most eminent degree, though they advert not [do not call attention] to virtue in particular; God, to whom they are united, carries them to the most extensive practice of it; he is exceedingly jealous over them, and prohibits them the taste of any pleasure but in himself.

What a hungering for sufferings have those souls, who thus glow with Divine Love! How prone to precipitate into excessive austerities, were they permitted to pursue their own inclinations! They think of nought save how they may please their Beloved: as their self-love abates, they neglect and forget themselves; and as their love to God increases, so do self-detestation and disregard to the creature.

O was this easy method acquired, a method so suited to all, to the dull and ignorant as well as to the acute and learned, how easily would the whole Church of God be reformed! Love only is required: "Love," saith S. Augustine, "and then do what you please." For when we truly love, we cannot have so much as a will to anything that might offend the Object of our affections.

CHAPTER 10

Of Mortification

I will even affirm, that, in any other way, it is next to an impossibility ever to acquire a perfect mortification of the senses and passions.

The reason is obvious; the soul gives vigor and energy to the senses, and the senses raise and stimulate the passions: a dead body has neither sensations nor passions, because its connection with the soul is dissolved.

All endeavors merely to rectify the exterior, impel the soul yet farther outward into that about which it is so warmly and zealously engaged. It is in these matters that its powers are diffused and scattered abroad: for its application being immediately directed to austerities, and other externals, it thus invigorates those very senses it is aiming to subdue. For the senses have no other spring from whence to derive their vigor, than the application of the soul to themselves; the degree of their life and activity is proportioned to the degree of attention which the soul bestows upon them; and this life of the senses stirs up and provokes the passions, instead of suppressing or subduing them: austerities may, indeed, enfeeble the body, but, for the reasons just mentioned, can never take off the keenness of the senses, or lessen their activity.

The only method to effect [bring about] this is inward recollection; by which the soul is turned wholly and altogether inward, to possess a Present God. If the soul directs all its vigor and energy towards this center of its being, the simple act separates and withdraws it from the senses; the exercising of all its powers internally leaves them faint and impotent; and the nearer it draws to God, the farther is it separated from the senses, and the less are the passions influenced by them.

Hence it is, that those in whom the attractions of grace are very powerful, find the outward man altogether weak and feeble, and even liable to faintings. I do not mean by this to discourage mortification; for it should ever accompany prayer, according to the strength and state of the person, or as obedience will allow. But I say that mortification should not be our principal exercise; nor should we prescribe ourselves such and such austerities, but follow simply and merely the internal attractions of grace; and being possessed and occupied with the Divine Presence (without thinking particularly on mortification) God will enable us to perform every species of it; and most assuredly he will give no relaxation to those who abide faithful in their abandonment to him, until he has mortified in them everything that remains to be mortified.

We have only then to continue steadfast in the utmost attention to God, and all things will be rightly performed. All are not capable of outward austerities, but all are capable of this. In the mortification of the eye and ear, which continually supply the busy imagination with new objects, there is little danger of falling into excess: but God will teach us this also, and we have only to follow where his Spirit guides.

The soul has a double advantage by proceeding thus, for, in withdrawing from outward objects, it draws the nearer to God; and in approaching him, besides the secret sustaining and preserving power and virtue received, it is the farther removed from sin, the nearer the approach is made; so that conversion becomes habitual.

CHAPTER 11

Of Conversion

Be ye truly converted unto that God from whom
ye have so deeply revolted.—Isa. 31:6

To be truly converted is to avert wholly from the creature, and turn wholly unto God.

For the attainment of salvation it is absolutely necessary that we should forsake outward sin and turn unto righteousness: but this alone is not perfect conversion, which consists in a total change of the whole man from an outward to an inward life.

When the soul is once turned to God a wonderful facility is found in continuing steadfast in conversion; and the longer it remains thus converted, the nearer it approaches, and the more firmly it adheres to God; and the nearer it draws to him, of necessity it is the farther removed from the creature, which is so contrary to him: so that it is so effectually established and rooted in its conversion that it becomes habitual, and, as it were, natural.

31

Now we must not suppose that this is effected by a violent exertion of its own powers; for it is not capable of, nor should it attempt any other co-operation with Divine Grace, than that of endeavoring to withdraw itself from external objects and to turn inwards: after which it has nothing farther to do than to continue steadfast in adherence to God.

God has an attractive virtue which draws the soul more and more powerfully to himself, the nearer it approaches towards him, and, in attracting, he purifies and refines it; just as with a gross vapor exhaled by the sun, which, as it gradually ascends, is rarified and rendered pure, the vapor, indeed, contributes to its exhalation only by its passiveness; but the soul co-operates with the attractions of God, by a free and affectionate correspondence. This kind of introversion is both easy and efficacious, advancing the soul naturally and without constraint, because God himself is its center.

Every center has a powerfully attractive virtue; and the more pure and exalted it is, the stronger and more irresistible are its attractions. But besides the potent magnetism of the center itself, there is, in every creature, a correspondent tendency to re-union with its peculiar center, which is vigorous and active in proportion to the spirituality and perfection of the subject.

As soon as anything is turned towards its center, its own gravitation instigates and accelerates it thereto, unless it be withheld by some invincible obstacle: a stone held in the hand is no sooner disengaged than by its own weight it falls to the earth as to its center; so also water and fire, when unobstructed, tend and flow incessantly to their principle or center. Now, when the soul, by its efforts to abandon outward objects, and gather itself inwards, is brought into the influence of this central tendency, without any other exertion, it falls gradually by the weight of Divine Love into its proper center; and the more passive and tranquil it remains, and the freer from self-motion and self-exertion, the more rapidly it advances, because the energy of the central attractive virtue is unobstructed and has full liberty for action.

All our care and attention should, therefore, be to acquire inward recollection: nor let us be discouraged by the pains and difficulties we encounter in this exercise, which will soon be recompensed, on the part of our God, by such abundant supplies of grace as will render the exercise perfectly easy, provided we be faithful in meekly withdrawing our hearts from outward distractions and occupations, and returning to our center with affections full of tenderness and serenity. When at any time the passions are turbulent, a gentle retreat inwards unto a Present God, easily deadens and pacifies them; and any other way of contending with them rather irritates than appeases them.

CHAPTER 12

Of the Presence of God

The soul that is faithful in the exercise of love and adherence to God above described, is astonished to feel him gradually taking possession of its whole being: it now enjoys a continual sense of that Presence, which is become, as it were, natural to it; and this, as well as prayer, is the result of habit. The soul feels an unusual serenity gradually being diffused throughout all its faculties; and silence now wholly constitutes its prayer; whilst God communicates an intuitive love, which is the beginning of ineffable blessedness. O that I were permitted to pursue this subject and describe some degrees of the endless progression of subsequent states![1] But I now write only for beginners; and shall, therefore, proceed no farther, but wait our Lord's time for publishing what may be applicable to every conceivable degree of "stature in Christ Jesus."

We must, however, urge it as a matter of the highest import, to cease from self-action and self-exertion, that God himself may act alone: he saith, by the mouth of his prophet David, "Be still, and know that I am God" (Ps. 46:10). But the creature is so infatuated with a love and attachment to its

---

[1] An idea pursued in the work entitled *Spiritual Torrents*, and also in *The Concise View*.

own workings, that it imagines nothing at all is done, if it doth not perceive and distinguish all its operations. It is ignorant that its inability to minutely observe the manner of its motion, is occasioned by the swiftness of its progress; and that the operations of God, in extending and diffusing their influence, absorb those of the creature. The stars may be seen distinctly before the sun rises; but as his light advances, their rays are gradually absorbed by his and they become invisible, not from the want of light in themselves, but from the superior effulgence of the chief luminary.

The case is similar here; for there is a strong and universal light which absorbs all the little distinct lights of the soul; they grow faint and disappear under its powerful influence, and self-activity is now no longer distinguishable. Yet those greatly err who accuse this prayer of idleness, a charge that can arise only from inexperience. If they would but make some efforts towards the attainment of this prayer, they would soon experience the contrary of what they suppose and find their accusation groundless.

This appearance of inaction is, indeed, not the consequence of sterility and want, but of fruitfulness and abundance, which will be clearly perceived by the experienced soul, who will know and feel that the silence is full and unctuous, and the result of causes totally the reverse of apathy and barrenness. There are two kinds of people that keep silence; the one because they have nothing to say, the other because they have too much: it is so with the soul in this state; the silence is occasioned by the superabundance of matter, too great for utterance.

To be drowned, and to die of thirst, are deaths widely different; yet water may, in some sense, be said to cause both; abundance destroys in one case, and want in the other. So in this state the abundance and overflowings of grace still the activity of self, and, therefore, it is of the utmost importance to remain as silent as possible.

The infant hanging at the mother's breast is a lively illustration of our subject: it begins to draw the milk by moving its little lips; but when the milk flows abundantly, it is content to swallow, and suspends its suction: by doing otherwise it would only hurt itself, spill the milk, and be obliged to quit the breast.

We must act in like manner in the beginning of Prayer, by exerting the lips of the affections; but as soon as the milk of Divine Grace flows freely, we have nothing to do but, in repose and stillness, sweetly to imbibe it; and when it ceases to flow, we must again stir up the affections as the infant moves its lips. Whoever acts otherwise cannot turn this grace to advantage, which is bestowed to allure and draw the soul into the repose of Love, and not into the multiplicity of Self.

But what becometh of this child, who gently and without motion drinketh in the milk? Who would believe that it can thus receive nourishment? Yet the more peacefully it feeds, the better it thrives. What, I say, becomes of this infant? It drops gently asleep on its mother's bosom. So the soul that is tranquil and peaceful in prayer, sinketh frequently into a mystic slumber, wherein all its powers are at rest; till at length it is wholly fitted for that state, of which it enjoys these transient anticipations. In this process the soul is led naturally, without effort, art, or study.

The Interior is not a stronghold to be taken by storm and violence, but a kingdom of peace, which is to be gained only by love.

If any will thus pursue the little path I have pointed out, it will lead them to intuitive prayer. God demands nothing extraordinary nor difficult; on the contrary, he is best pleased by a simple and child-like conduct.

That which is most sublime and elevated in religion is the easiest attained: the most necessary sacraments are the least difficult. It is thus also in natural things: if you would go to sea, embark on a river, and you will be conveyed to it insensibly and without exertion. Would you go to God, follow this sweet and simple path, and you will arrive at the desired object, with an ease and expedition that will amaze you.

O that you would but once make the trial! How soon would you find that all I have advanced falls short of the reality, and that your own experience will carry you infinitely beyond it! Is it fear that prevents you from instantly casting yourself into those arms of Love, which were widely extended on the Cross only to receive you? Whence can your fears arise? What risk do you run, in depending solely on your God, and abandoning yourself wholly unto him? Ah! he will not deceive you, unless by bestowing an abundance beyond your highest hopes: but those who expect all from themselves will inevitably be deceived, and must suffer this rebuke of God by his prophet Isaiah, "Ye have wearied yourselves in the multiplicity of your ways, and have not said let us rest in peace" (Isa. 57:10, Vulgate).

CHAPTER 13

Of Rest Before God

The soul advanced thus far hath no need of any other preparation than its quietude: for now the Presence of God, which is the great effect, or rather continuation of Prayer, begins to be infused, and almost without intermission. The soul enjoys transcendent blessedness, and feels that "it no longer lives, but that Christ liveth in it"; and that the only way to find him is introversion. No sooner do the bodily eyes close than the soul is wrapt up in Prayer: it is amazed at so great a blessing, and enjoys an internal converse, which external matters cannot interrupt.

The same may be said of this species of prayer that is said of wisdom, "all good things come together with her" (Wisdom 7:11). For the virtues flow from this soul into exertion with so much sweetness and facility that they appear natural and spontaneous; and the living spring within breaks forth so freely and abundantly into all goodness that it becomes even insensible to evil. Let it then remain faithful in this state; and beware of choosing or seeking any other disposition whatsoever than this simple rest as a preparative either to Confession or Communion, to action or prayer, for its sole business is to expand itself for the full reception of the Divine infusions. I would not be understood to speak of the preparations necessary for the sacraments, but of the most perfect dispositions in which they can be received.

CHAPTER 14

Of Inward Silence

The Lord is in his holy temple:
let all the earth keep silence before him.—Hab. 2:20

Inward silence is absolutely indispensable, because the Word is essential and eternal, and necessarily requires dispositions in the soul in some degree correspondent to his nature, as a capacity for the reception of himself. Hearing is a sense formed to receive sounds, and is rather passive than active, admitting, but not communicating sensation; and if we would hear, we must lend the ear for that purpose: so Christ, the eternal Word, without whose Divine in-speaking the soul is dead, dark, and barren, when he would speak within us, requires the most silent attention to his all-quickening and efficacious voice.

Hence it is so frequently enjoined us in sacred writ, to hear and be attentive to the Voice of God. Of the numerous exhortations to this effect I shall quote a few: "Hearken unto me, my people, and give ear unto me, O my nation" (Isa. 41:4), and again, "Hear me, all ye whom I carry in my bosom, and bear within my bowels" (Isa. 46:3), and farther by the Psalmist,

> Hearken, O daughter, and consider, and incline thine ear; forget also thine own people, and thy father's house; so shall the King greatly desire thy beauty. (Psa. 45:10, 11)

We should forget ourselves, and all self-interest, and listen and be attentive to the voice of our God: and these two simple actions, or rather passive dispositions, attract his love to that beauty which he himself communicates.

Outward silence is very requisite for the cultivation and improvement of inward; and indeed it is impossible we should become truly internal without the love and practice of outward silence and retirement. God saith, by the mouth of his prophet, "I will lead her into solitude, and there will I speak to her heart" (Hos. 2:14, Vulgate); and unquestionably the being internally occupied and engaged with God is wholly incompatible with being busied and employed in the numerous trifles that surround us (Luke 38:42).

When through imbecility or unfaithfulness we become dissipated, or as it were, uncentered, it is of immediate importance to turn again gently and sweetly inward; and thus we may learn to preserve the spirit and unction of prayer throughout the day; for if prayer and recollection were wholly confined to any appointed half-hour or hour, we should reap but little fruit.

CHAPTER 15

Of Confession and Self-Examination

Self-examination should always precede Confession, and in the nature and manner of it should be conformable to the state of the soul: the business of those that are advanced to the degree of which we now treat, is to lay their whole souls open before God, who will not fail to enlighten them, and enable them to see the peculiar nature of their faults. This examination, however, should be peaceful and tranquil, and we should depend on God for the discovery and knowledge of our sins, rather than on the diligence of our own scrutiny.

When we examine with constraint, and in the strength of our own endeavors, we are easily deceived and betrayed by self-love into error; "we believe the evil good, and the good evil" (Isa. 5:20); but when we lie in full exposure before the Sun of Righteousness, his divine beams render the smallest atoms visible. It follows from hence that we must forsake self, and abandon our souls to God as well in examination as Confession.

When souls have attained to this species of prayer no fault escapes reprehension; on every commission they are instantly rebuked by an inward

41

burning and tender confusion. Such is the scrutiny of him who suffers no evil to be concealed; and under his purifying influence the one way is to turn affectionately to our Judge, and bear with meekness the pain and correction he inflicts. He becomes the incessant Examiner of the soul; it can now, indeed, no longer examine itself, and if it be faithful in its resignation, experience will convince the soul that it is a thousand times more effectually examined by his Divine Light than by the most active and vigorous self-inspection.

Those who tread these paths should be informed of a matter respecting their Confession in which they are apt to err. When they begin to give an account of their sins, instead of the regret and contrition they had been accustomed to feel, they find that love and tranquility sweetly pervade and take possession of their souls. Now those who are not properly instructed are desirous of withdrawing from this sensation, to form an act of contrition, because they have heard, and with truth, that it is requisite. But they are not aware that they lose thereby the genuine contrition, which is this Intuitive Love, infinitely surpassing any effect produced by self-exertion, and comprehending the other acts in itself as in one principal act, in much higher perfection than if they were distinctly perceived, and varied in their sensation. Be not then troubled about other things when God acts so excellently in you and for you.

To hate sin in this manner is to hate it as God does. The purest love is that which is of his immediate operation in the soul: why should it then be so eager for action? Let it remain in the state he assigns it, agreeable to the instructions of Solomon: "Put your confidence in God; remain in quiet, where he hath placed you" (Eccles. 11:22).

The soul will also be amazed at finding a difficulty in calling faults to remembrance: this, however, should cause no uneasiness; first, because this forgetfulness of our faults is some proof of our purification from them; and in this degree of advancement it is best. Secondly, because when Confession is our duty, God will not fail to make known to us our greatest faults, for then he himself examines, and the soul will feel the end of examination more perfectly accomplished than it could possibly have been by the utmost exertion of its own endeavors.

These instructions, however, would be altogether unsuitable to the preceding degrees while the soul continues in its active state, wherein it is right and necessary it should in all things use the utmost industry in proportion to the degree of its advancement. It is those that have arrived at this more advanced state whom I would exhort to follow these instructions, and not to vary their one simple occupation even on approaching the Communion; they should remain in silence, and suffer God to act freely and without limitation. Who can better receive the Body and Blood of Christ than he in whom the Holy Spirit is indwelling?

Chapter 16

Of Reading and Vocal Prayer

If, while reading, you feel yourself recollected, lay aside the book and remain in stillness; at all times read but little, and cease to read when you are thus internally attracted.

The soul that is called to a state of inward silence should not encumber itself with long vocal prayers; whenever it does pray vocally, and finds a difficulty therein, and an attraction to silence, it should not use constraint by persevering, but yield to the internal drawings, unless the repeating such prayers be a matter of obedience. In any other case, it is much better not to be burdened with and tied down to the repetition of set forms, but wholly given up to the leadings of the Holy Spirit; and herein, indeed, is every species of devotion inclusively fulfilled in a most eminent degree.

CHAPTER 17

Of Petitions

The soul should not be surprised at feeling itself unable to offer up to God such petitions as it had formerly made with freedom and facility; for now the Spirit maketh intercession for it according to the will of God, that

> Spirit which helpeth our infirmities: for we know not what we should pray for as we ought; but the Spirit itself maketh intercession for us, with groanings which cannot be uttered. (Rom. 8:26)

We must co-operate with, and second the designs of God, which tend to divest us of all our own operations, that in the place thereof his own may be substituted. Let this then be done in you, and suffer not yourself to be attached to anything, however good it may appear; for it is no longer good if it in any measure turns you aside from that which God willeth of you: the Divine Will is preferable to all things else. Shake off then all attachments to the interests of self, and live on faith and resignation; here it is that genuine faith begins truly to operate.

Chapter 18

Of Defects or Infirmities

Should we wander among externals, or sink into dissipation, or commit a fault, we must instantly turn inwards; for having departed thereby from our God, we should as soon as possible return again unto him, and suffer in his presence whatever sensations he is pleased to impress. On the commission of a fault, it is of great importance to guard against vexation and disquietude, which springs from a secret root of pride and a love of our own excellence. We are hurt by feeling what we are; and if we discourage ourselves or despond, we are the more enfeebled; and from our reflections on the fault a chagrin arises, which is often worse than the fault itself.

The truly humble soul is not surprised at defects or failings; and the more miserable and wretched it beholds itself, the more doth it abandon itself unto God, and press for a nearer and more intimate alliance with him, that it may avail itself of his eternal strength. We should rather be induced to act thus, as God himself hath said, "I will make thee understand what thou oughtest to do; I will teach thee the way by which thou shouldst go; and I will have mine eye continually upon thee for a guide" (Psa. 32:8, Vulgate).

CHAPTER 19

Of Distractions and Temptations

A direct contest and struggle with distractions and temptations rather serves to augment them, and withdraws the soul from that adherence to God, which should ever be its principal occupation.

The surest and safest method for conquest is simply to turn away from the evil and draw yet nearer and closer to our God. A little child, on perceiving a monster, does not wait to fight with it, and will scarcely turn its eyes towards it, but quickly shrinks into the bosom of its mother, in total confidence of safety; so likewise should the soul turn from the dangers of temptation to God. "God is in the midst of her," saith the Psalmist, "she shall not be moved; God shall help her, and that right early" (Psa. 46:5).

If we do otherwise, and in our weakness attempt to attack our enemies, we shall frequently feel ourselves wounded, if not totally defeated; but, by casting ourselves into the simple Presence of God, we shall find instant supplies of strength for our support.

47

This was the succor sought for by David: "I have set," saith he,

the Lord always before me: because he is at my right hand, I shall not be moved. Therefore my heart is glad, and my glory rejoiceth: my flesh also shall rest in hope. (Psa. 16:8, 9)

And it is said in Exodus, "The Lord shall fight for you, and ye shall hold your peace."

CHAPTER 20

Of Self-Annihilation

Supplication and sacrifice are comprehended in prayer, which, according to S. John, is "an incense, the smoke whereof ascendeth unto God;" therefore it is said in the Apocalypse that "unto the Angel was given much incense, that he should offer it with the prayers of all Saints" (Rev. 8:3).

Prayer is the effusion of the heart in the Presence of God: "I have poured out my soul before God" saith the mother of Samuel. (1 Sam. 1:15) The prayer of the wise men at the feet of Christ in the stable of Bethlehem, was signified by the incense they offered: for prayer being the energy and fire of love, melting, dissolving, and sublimating the soul, and causing it to ascend unto God; therefore, in proportion as the soul is melted and dissolved, in like proportion do odors issue from it; and these odors proceed from the intense fire of love within.

This is illustrated in the Canticles (1:11) where the spouse saith, "While the King sitteth on his couch, my spikenard sendeth forth the smell thereof." The couch is the ground or center of the soul; and when

49

God is there, and we know how to dwell with him, and abide in his Presence, the sacred power and influence thereof gradually dissolves the obduration [hardening] of the soul, and, as it melteth, odors issue forth: hence it is, that the Beloved saith of his spouse, in seeing her soul melt when he spake, "Who is this that cometh out of the wilderness, like pillars of smoke perfumed with myrrh and frankincense?" (Cant. 5:6 and 3:6).

Thus doth the soul ascend unto God, by giving up self to the destroying and annihilating power of Divine Love: this, indeed, is a most essential and necessary sacrifice in the Christian religion, and that alone by which we pay true homage to the sovereignty of God; as it is written, "The power of the Lord is great, and he is honored only by the humble" (Eccles. 3:20). By the destruction of the existence of self within us, we truly acknowledge the supreme existence of our God; for unless we cease to exist in self, the Spirit of the Eternal Word cannot exist in us. Now it is by the giving up of our own life, that we give place for his coming; and "in dying to ourselves, he liveth and abideth in us."

We should, indeed, surrender our whole being unto Christ Jesus: and cease to live any longer in ourselves, that he may become our life; "that being dead, our life may be hid with Christ in God" (Col. 3:3). "Pass ye into me," saith God, "all ye who earnestly seek after me" (Eccles. 24:16). But how is it we pass into God? We leave and forsake ourselves, that we may be lost in him; and this can be effected [accomplished] only by annihilation; which, being the true prayer of adoration, renders unto God alone, all "Blessing, honor, glory and power, for ever and ever" (Rev. 5:13).

This is the prayer of truth; "It is worshiping God in spirit and in truth" (John 4:23). "In spirit," because we enter into the purity of that Spirit which prayeth within us, and are drawn forth and freed from our own carnal and corrupt manner of praying; "In truth" because we are thereby placed in the great Truth of the All of God, and the Nothing of the creature.

There are but these two truths, the All, and the Nothing; everything else is falsehood. We can pay due honor to the All of God, only in our own annihilation, which is no sooner accomplished, than he, who never suffers a void in nature, instantly fills us with himself.

Did we but know the virtue and the blessings which the soul derives from this prayer, we should willingly be employed therein without ceasing.

"It is the pearl of great price: it is the hidden treasure" (Matt. 13:44, 45), which, whoever findeth, selleth freely all that he hath to purchase it. "It is the well of living water, which springeth up unto everlasting life." It is the adoration of God "in spirit and in truth" (John 4:14–23), and it is the full performance of the purest evangelical precepts.

Jesus Christ assureth us, that the "Kingdom of God is within us" (Luke 17:21), and this is true in two senses. First, when God becometh so fully the Master and Lord in us, that nothing resisteth his dominion; then is our interior his kingdom. And again, when we possess God, who is the Supreme Good, we possess his kingdom also, wherein there is fullness of joy, and where we attain the end of our creation: thus it is said, "to serve God, is to reign." The end of our creation, indeed, is to enjoy our God, even in this life; but alas! how few there are who think of this seriously.

Chapter 21

The Noble Results of this Species of Prayer

Some persons, when they hear of the prayer of silence, falsely imagine, that the soul remains stupid, dead, and inactive. But, unquestionably, it acteth therein, more nobly and more extensively than it had ever done before; for God himself is the mover, and the soul now acteth by the agency of his Spirit.

When S. Paul speaks of our being led by the Spirit of God, it is not meant that we should cease from action; but that we should act through the internal agency of his Grace. This is finely represented by the prophet Ezekiel's vision of the

> wheels, which had a Living Spirit; and whithersoever the Spirit was to go, they went; they ascended, and descended, as they were moved; for the Spirit of Life was in them, and they returned not when they went. (Ezek. 1:18)

Thus the soul should be equally subservient to the will of that Vivifying [life-bringing] Spirit wherewith it is informed, and [be] scrupulously faithful to follow only as that moves. These motions now never tend to return, in reflection on the creatures or itself; but go forward, in an incessant approach towards the chief end.

This action of the soul is attended with the utmost tranquility. When it acts of itself, the act is forced and constrained; and, therefore, it can the more easily perceive and distinguish it: but when it acteth under the influence of the Spirit of Grace, its action is so free, so easy, and so natural, that it almost seems as if it did not act at all: "he hath set me at large, he hath delivered me, because he delighted in me" (Psa. 18:19).

When the soul is in its central tendency (or, in other words, is returned through recollection into itself), from that moment the central attraction becomes a most potent action, infinitely surpassing in its energy every other species. Nothing, indeed, can equal the swiftness of this tendency to the center: and though an action, yet it is so noble, so peaceful, so full of tranquility, so natural and spontaneous, that it appears to the soul as if it did not act at all.

When a wheel rolls slowly we can easily distinguish its parts; but when its motion is rapid we can distinguish nothing. So the soul, which rests in God, hath an activity exceedingly noble and elevated, yet altogether peaceful: and the more peaceful it is, the swifter is its course; because it is proportionately given up to that Spirit, by which it is moved and directed.

This attracting spirit is no other than God himself, who, in drawing us, causes us to run unto him. How well did the spouse understand this when she said, "Draw me, and we will run after thee" (Cant. 1:3). Draw me unto thee, O my divine center, by the secret springs of my existence, and all my powers and senses shall follow the potent magnetism! This simple attraction is both an ointment to heal, and a perfume to allure: "we follow," saith she, "the fragrance of thy perfumes"; and though so powerfully magnetic, it is followed by the soul freely, and without constraint; for it is equally delightful as forcible; and whilst it attracts by its potency, it charms with its sweetness. "Draw me," saith the spouse, "and we will run after Thee." She speaketh of and to herself: "draw me,"—behold the unity of the center, which attracteth! "We will run,"—behold the correspondence and course of all the senses and powers in following that attraction!

Instead then of promoting idleness, we promote the highest activity by inculcating a total dependence on the Spirit of God as our moving principle; for it is "in him we live, and move, and have our being" (Acts 17:28). This meek dependence on the Spirit of God is indispensably necessary to reinstate the soul in its primeval unity and simplicity, that it may thereby attain the end of its creation.

We must, therefore, forsake our multifarious activity, to re-enter the simplicity and unity of God, in whose image we were originally formed. "The Spirit is one and manifold" (Wisdom 7:22), and his unity doth not preclude his multiplicity. We enter into his unity when we are united unto his Spirit, and have one and the same Spirit with him; and we are multiplied in respect to the outward execution of his will, without any departure from our state of union: so that when we are wholly moved by the Divine Spirit, which is infinitely active, our activity must, indeed, differ widely in its energy and degree from that which is merely our own.

We must yield ourselves to the guidance of "Wisdom, which is more moving than any motion" (Wisdom 7:24); and by abiding in dependence on its action, our activity will be truly efficient. "All things were made by the Word, and without him was not anything made, that was made" (John 1:3). God originally formed us in his own likeness; and he now informeth us with the Spirit of his Word, that "Breath of Life" (Gen. 2:7), which was inbreathed at our creation, in the participation whereof the Image of God consisted; and this life is a Life of Unity, simple, pure, intimate, and always fruitful. The Devil having broken and deformed the Divine Image in the soul, the agency of the same Word, whose Spirit was inbreathed at our creation, is absolutely necessary for its renovation; and it can only be renewed by our being passive under him who is to renew it. But who can restore the Image of God within us in its primeval form, save he who is the Essential Image of the Father?

Our activity should, therefore, consist in endeavoring to acquire and maintain such a state as may be most susceptible of divine impressions, most flexile to all the operations of the Eternal Word. Whilst a tablet is unsteady, the painter is unable to delineate a true copy: so every act of our own selfish and proper spirit is productive of false and erroneous lineaments; it interrupts the work, and defeats the design of this adorable Painter; we must then remain in peace and move only when he moves us. "Jesus Christ hath the Life, in himself" (John 5:26), and he should be the life of every living thing.

As all action is estimable only in proportion to the dignity of the efficient principle, this action is incontestably more noble than any other. Actions produced by a divine principle, are divine; but creaturely actions, however good they appear, are only human, or at best virtuous, even when accompanied by Grace. Jesus Christ saith, he hath the Life in himself. All other beings have only a borrowed life; but the Word hath the Life in himself, and being communicative of his nature he desireth to communicate it to man. We should, therefore, make room for the influx of this Life, which can only be done by the ejection of the Adamical life, the suppression of the activity of self. This is agreeable to the assertion of S. Paul: "If any man be in Christ he is a new creature: old things are passed away; behold all things are become new!" (2 Cor. 5:17), but this state can be accomplished only by dying to ourselves and to all our own activity, that the activity of God may be substituted in its place.

Instead, therefore, of prohibiting activity, we enjoin it; but in absolute dependence on the Spirit of God, that his activity may take place of our own. This can only be effected by the concurrence of the creature; and this concurrence can only be yielded by moderating and restraining our own activity, that the activity of God may gradually gain the ascendancy, and finally absorb all that is ours as distinguishable from it.

Jesus Christ hath exemplified this in the gospel. Martha did what was right; but because she did it in her own spirit, Christ rebuked her. The spirit of man is restless and turbulent; for which reason it does little, though it would appear to do much. "Martha," saith Christ,

> thou art careful and troubled about many things, but one thing is needful; and Mary hath chosen that good part which shall not be taken away from her. (Luke 10:41–42)

And what was it that Mary had chosen? Repose, tranquility, and peace. She apparently ceased to act, that the Spirit of Christ might act in her; she ceased to live, that Christ might be her life.

This shows us how necessary it is to renounce ourselves and all our own activity, to follow Jesus Christ—and we cannot follow him without being animated with his Spirit. Now that his Spirit may gain admission in us, it is necessary that our own proper spirit should be first expelled: "he that is joined unto the Lord," saith S. Paul, "is one spirit with him" (1 Cor. 6:17); and David said, "It was good for him to draw near unto the Lord, and to put his trust in him" (Ps. 73:28). This drawing near unto God, is the beginning of Union.

Divine Union has its commencement, its progression, and its consummation. It is first an inclination and tendency towards God: when the soul is introverted in the manner before described, it gets within the influence of the central attraction, and acquires an eager desire after Union: on a nearer approach unto God, it adheres to him; and growing stronger and stronger in its adhesion, it finally becomes one; that is, "One Spirit with him:" and it is thus that the spirit which had wandered and strayed from God, returns again to its proper source.

Into this process, which is the divine motion, and the spirit of Jesus Christ, we must necessarily enter. S. Paul saith, "If any man hath not the spirit of Christ, he is none of his" (Rom. 8:9): therefore, to be Christ's, we must be filled with his Spirit, and to be filled with his Spirit we must be emptied of our own. The apostle, in the same passage, proves the necessity of this divine influence or motion: "As many" saith he, "as are led by the spirit of God, they are the sons of God" (Rom. 8:14). The Spirit of Divine Filiation[1] is then the Spirit of Divine action or motion: he, therefore, adds, "Ye have not received the spirit of bondage again to fear; but ye have received the Spirit of Adoption, whereby we, cry, 'Abba, Father.'"

This Spirit is no other than the Spirit of Christ, through which we participate in his Filiation. "And this Spirit beareth witness with our spirit, that we are the children of God" (Rom. 8:16). When the soul yields itself to the influence and motions of this Blessed Spirit, it feels the testimony of its Divine Filiation; and it feels also, with superadded [added over and above] joy, that it hath received not the Spirit of bondage, but of liberty, even the liberty of the children of God. It then finds that it acts freely and sweetly, though with vigor and infallibility.

---

[1] Filiation: The condition or fact of being the child of a certain parent. (*American Heritage Dictionary*, 2000.)

The Spirit of Divine Action is so necessary in all things, that S. Paul, in the same passage, foundeth that necessity on our ignorance with respect to what we pray for: "The Spirit," saith he,

> also helpeth our infirmities: for we know not what we should pray for as we ought; but the Spirit itself maketh intercession for us, with groanings which cannot be uttered.

This is positive; if we know not what we stand in need of, nor pray, as we ought to do, for those things which are necessary; and if the Spirit which is in us, and to which we resign ourselves, asks and intercedes for us; should we not give unlimited freedom to its action, to its ineffable groanings in our behalf?

This Spirit is the Spirit of the Word, which is always heard, as he [Jesus] saith himself: "I know that thou hearest me always" (John 11:42); and if we freely admit this Spirit to pray and intercede in us, we also shall be always heard. The reason of this is given us by the same apostle, that skillful mystic, and master of the Internal life, where he adds,

> he that searcheth the heart, knoweth what is the mind of the Spirit; because he maketh intercession for the saints, according to the will of God. (Rom. 8:27)

That is to say, the Spirit demandeth only that which is conformable to the will of God; and the will of God is, that we should be saved: that we should become perfect. He [the Spirit], therefore, intercedeth for that which is necessary for so great an end.

Why should we then burden ourselves with superfluous cares, and fatigue and weary ourselves in the multiplicity of our ways, without ever saying, "Let us rest in peace?" God himself inviteth us to cast our cares, our anxieties, upon him. He complains in Isaiah, with ineffable goodness, that the soul had expended its powers and its treasures on a thousand external objects, and mistook its path to happiness, which was attainable by means much more facile [easy]: "Wherefore," saith God,

> do you spend money for that which is not bread? And your labor for that which satisfieth not? Hearken diligently unto me, and eat ye that which is good, and let your soul delight itself in fatness. (Isa. 45:2)

Did we but know the blessedness of thus hearkening unto God, and how greatly the soul is strengthened and invigorated thereby, "All flesh would surely be silent before the Lord" (Zech. 2:13); all would cease and be still, as soon as he appears. But to engage us farther in a boundless resignation, God assures us, by the same prophet, that we should fear nothing in this abandonment, because he takes a care of us, surpassing the highest tenderness of which we can form an idea. "Can a woman" saith he,

> forget her sucking child, that she should not have compassion on the son of her womb? Yea, she may forget; yet will I not forget thee. (Isa. 49:15)

O blessed assurance, pregnant with consolation! Who, after this, shall be fearful of resigning themselves wholly to the dispensations and guidance of their God?

Chapter 22

Of Internal Acts

Acts are distinguished into External and Internal. External acts are those which bear relation to some sensible object, and are either morally good or evil, merely according to the nature of the principle from which they proceed. I intend here to speak only of Internal acts, those energies of the soul, by which it turns internally to some objects, and averts from others.

If during my application to God I should form a will to change the nature of my act, I thereby withdraw myself from God, and turn to created objects, and that in a greater or less degree according to the strength of the act: and if, when I am turned towards the creature, I would return to God, I must necessarily form an act for that purpose; and the more perfect this act is, the more complete is the conversion.

Till conversion is perfected, many reiterated acts are necessary; for it is generally progressive, though with some it is almost instantaneous. My act, however, should consist in a continual turning unto God, an exertion of every faculty and power of the soul purely for him, agreeably to the instructions of the Son of Sirach: "Re-unite all the motions of thy heart in the holiness of God," and to the example of David, "I will keep my whole strength for thee" (Ps. 58:10), which is done by earnestly re-entering into one's self. As Isaiah saith, "Return to your heart" (Isa. 46:8); for we have strayed from our heart by sin, and it is our heart only that God requires: "My son, give me thine heart, and let thine eye observe my ways" (Prov. 23:26). To give the heart to God is to have the whole eternal energy of the soul ever centering in him, that we may be rendered conformable to his will. We must, therefore, continue invariably turned to God from our very first application to him.

But the soul, being weak and unstable, and accustomed to turn to external objects, is consequently prone to dissipation. This evil, however, will be counteracted if the soul, on perceiving the aberration, by a pure act of return to God, instantly re-places itself again in him; and this act subsists as long as the conversion by the powerful influence of a simple and unfeigned return to God lasts: and as many reiterated acts form a habit, the soul contracts the habit of conversion, and that act which was before interrupted and distinct becomes continual.

The soul should not then be perplexed about forming an act which already subsists, and which, indeed, it cannot attempt to form without difficulty and constraint. It even finds that it is withdrawn from its proper state under pretense of seeking that which is, in reality, acquired, seeing the habit is already formed and is confirmed in habitual conversion and habitual love. It is seeking one act by the help of many, instead of continuing attached to God by one simple act alone.

We may remark that at times we form with facility many distinct yet simple acts, which shows that we have wandered, and that we re-enter our heart after having strayed from it; yet when we have re-entered, we should remain there in peace. We err, therefore, in supposing that we do not form acts; we form them continually, but they should be in their nature conformable to the degree of our spiritual advancement.

The greatest difficulty with most spiritual people arises from their not clearly comprehending this matter. Now some acts are transient and distinct, others are continual; and again, some are direct, and others reflex [reflective]. All cannot form the first, neither are all in a state suited to form the last. The first are adapted to those who have strayed, and who require a distinguishable exertion, proportioned to the degree of their deviation, which, if inconsiderable, an act of the most simple kind is sufficient.

By the continued act I mean that [act] whereby the soul is altogether turned toward God in a direct tendency, which always subsists, and which it doth not renew unless it has been interrupted. The soul being thus turned is in charity, and abides therein, "and he that dwelleth in love dwelleth in God"(1 John 4:16). The soul then, as it were, existeth and reposeth in this habitual act, but free from sloth or torpor; for still there is an unintermitted act subsisting, which is a sweet sinking into the Deity, whose attraction becomes more and more powerful; and in following this potent attraction, the soul presses farther, and sinks continually deeper, into the ocean of Divine Love, maintaining an activity infinitely more powerful, vigorous, and effectual than that which served to accomplish its first return.

Now the soul that is thus profoundly and vigorously active, [because it is] being wholly given up to God, doth not perceive its activity, because it is direct and not reflex; and this is the cause why some, who do not express themselves properly, say that they do not act at all. But it is a mistake, for they were never more truly or nobly active: they should rather say that they did not distinguish their acts, than that they did not act. I allow they do not act of themselves, but they are drawn, and they follow the attraction. Love is the weight which sinks them into God, as into an infinite sea, wherein they descend with inconceivable rapidity from one profound depth to another.

It is then an impropriety to say that we do not form acts: all form acts, but the manner of their formation is not alike in all. The cause of the mistake is this, all who know they should act, are desirous of acting distinguishably and perceptibly. But this cannot be; distinct and sensible acts are for beginners, and acts of a higher nature for those in a more advanced state. To stop in the former, which are weak and of little profit, is to debar one's self of the latter; and again, to attempt the latter without having passed through the former is a no less considerable error.

All things should then be done in their season. Every state has its commencement, its progress, and its consummation; and it is an unhappy error to stop in the beginning. There is even no art but what hath its progress; and at first we must labor with diligence and toil, but at last we shall reap the harvest of our industry. When the vessel is in port the mariners are obliged to exert all their strength that they may clear her thence and put to sea; but at length they turn her with facility as they please. In like manner, while the soul remains in sin and creaturely entanglements, very frequent and strenuous endeavors are requisite to effect its freedom; the cords which withhold it must be loosed; and then by strong and vigorous efforts it gathers itself inwards, pushing off gradually from the old port; and in leaving that at a distance it proceeds to the interior, the haven to which it wishes to steer.

When the vessel is thus turned, in proportion as she advances on the sea, she leaves the land behind; and the farther she departs from the old harbor, the less difficulty and labor is requisite in moving her forward: at length she begins to get sweetly under sail and now proceeds so swiftly in her course that the oars which have become useless are laid aside. How is the pilot now employed? He is content with spreading the sails and holding the rudder. To spread the sails is to lay one's self before God in the prayer of simple exposition, that we may be acted upon by his Spirit: to hold the rudder is to restrain our hearts from wandering from the true course, recalling it gently, and guiding it steadily to the dictates of the blessed Spirit, which gradually gain possession and dominion of the heart, just as the wind by degrees fills the sails and impels the vessel. While the winds are fair the pilot and mariners rest from their labors, and the vessel glides rapidly along without their toil; and when they thus repose and leave the vessel to the wind, they make more way in one hour than they had done in a length of time by all their former efforts: were they even now to attempt using the oar they would not only fatigue themselves, but retard the vessel by their ill-timed labors.

This is the manner of acting we should pursue interiorly; it will, indeed, advance us in a short time, by the divine impulsion, infinitely farther than a whole life spent in reiterated acts of self-exertion; and whosoever will take this path will find it easier than any other.

If the wind is contrary and blows a storm, we must cast anchor to withhold the vessel: our anchor is a firm confidence and hope in our God, waiting patiently the calming of the tempest and the return of a favorable gale as David waited patiently for the Lord, and he inclined unto him and heard his cry (Ps. 40:1). We must, therefore, be resigned to the Spirit of God, giving up ourselves wholly to his Divine Guidance.

Chapter 23

To Pastors and Teachers

If all who labored for the conversion of others were to introduce them immediately into Prayer and the Interior Life and make it their main design to gain and win over the heart, numberless as well as permanent conversions would certainly ensue. On the contrary, few and transient fruits must attend that labor which is confined to outward matters; such as burdening the disciple with a thousand precepts for external exercises, instead of leaving the soul to Christ by the occupation of the heart in him.

If ministers were solicitous thus to instruct their parishioners; shepherds, while they watched their flocks, might have the Spirit of the primitive Christians, and the husbandman at the plough maintain a blessed intercourse with his God; the manufacturer, while he exhausts his outward man with labor, would be renewed in internal strength; and every species of vice would shortly disappear and every parishioner become a true follower of the Good Shepherd.

O when once the heart is gained, how easily is all moral evil corrected! It is, therefore, that God, above all things, requires the *heart*. It is

63

the conquest of the heart alone that can extirpate those dreadful vices which are so predominant, such as drunkenness, blasphemy, lewdness, envy, and theft. Jesus Christ would become the universal and peaceful Sovereign, and the face of the Church would be wholly renewed.

The decay of internal piety is unquestionably the source of the various errors that have arisen in the Church; all which would speedily be sapped and overthrown should inward religion be re-established. Errors are only so far prejudicial to the soul as they tend to weaken faith and deter from prayer; and if, instead of engaging our wandering brethren in vain disputes, we could but teach them simply to believe and diligently to pray, we should lead them sweetly unto God.

O how inexpressibly great is the loss sustained by mankind from the neglect of the Interior Life! And how tremendous must the great day of retribution be to those who are entrusted with the care of souls, for not having discovered and dispensed to their flock this hidden treasure.

Some excuse themselves by saying that this is a dangerous way; pleading the incapacity of simple persons to comprehend spiritual matters. But the Oracles of Truth affirm the contrary: "The Lord loveth those who walk simply" (Prov. 12:22). And where can be the danger of walking in the only true way, which is Jesus Christ? Of giving up ourselves to him, fixing our eye continually upon him, placing all our confidence in his grace, and tending with all the strength of our soul to his pure Love?

The simple ones, so far from being incapable of this perfection, are, by their docility, innocence, and humility, peculiarly adapted and qualified for its attainment; and as they are not accustomed to reasoning, they are less employed in speculations, less tenacious of their own opinions. Even from their want of learning, they submit more freely to the teachings of the Divine Spirit: whereas others, who are blinded by self-sufficiency and enslaved by prejudice, give great resistance to the operations of grace.

We are told in Scripture "that unto the simple, God giveth the understanding of his law" (Ps. 118:130); and we are also assured that God loveth to commune freely with them: "The Lord careth for the simple; I was reduced to extremity, and he saved me" (Ps. 114:6). To warn spiritual fathers against preventing the little ones from coming to Christ, he himself said to his apostles, "Suffer little children to come unto me, for of such is the kingdom of Heaven" (Matt. 19:14). It was the endeavor of the Apostles to prevent children from going to our Lord, which occasioned this gracious charge. Man frequently applies a remedy to the outward body, whilst the disease lies at the heart.

The cause of our being so unsuccessful in reforming mankind, especially those of the lower class, is our beginning with external matters. All our labors in this field do but produce such fruit as endures not: but if the key of the interior be first given, the exterior would be naturally and easily reformed. To teach man to seek God in his heart, to think of him, to return to Him whenever he finds that He has wandered from him, and to do and to suffer all things with a single eye to please Him, is the natural and ready process; it is leading the soul to the very source of Grace, wherein is to be found all that is necessary for sanctification.

I, therefore, conjure you all, O ye who have the care of souls, to put them at once into this way, which is Jesus Christ; nay, it is he himself who conjures you, by the Precious Blood he hath shed for those entrusted to you, "to speak to the heart of Jerusalem" (Isa. 40:2). O ye dispensers of his grace, ye preachers of his Word, ye ministers of his Sacraments, establish his kingdom!—and that it may indeed be established, make him ruler over the hearts of his subjects! For as it is the heart alone that can oppose his Sovereignty, it is by the subjection of the heart that his Sovereignty is most highly exalted: "Give glory to the holiness of God, and he shall become your sanctification" (Isa. 8:13). Compose catechisms particularly to teach prayer, not by reasoning nor by method, for the simple are incapable thereof; but to teach the prayer of the heart, not of the understanding; the prayer of God's Spirit, not of man's invention.

Alas! By wanting them to pray in elaborate forms, and to be curiously critical therein, you create their chief obstacles. The children have been led astray from the best of Fathers, by your endeavoring to teach them too refined, too polished a language. Go then, ye poor children, to your heavenly Father; speak to him in your natural language; and though it be ever so rude and barbarous in the opinion of men, it is not so to him. A father is much better pleased with an address which love and respect in the child throws into disorder, because he knows it proceeds from the heart, than by a formal and barren harangue, though ever so elaborate in the composition. The simple and undisguised emotions of filial love are infinitely more expressive than all language and all reasoning.

By forming instructions how to love the Essential Love by rule and method, men have in a great measure estranged themselves from him. O how unnecessary is it to teach an art of loving! The language of Love, though natural to the lover, is nonsense and barbarism to him who loveth not. The best way to learn the love of God is to love him. The ignorant and simple, because they proceed with more cordiality and simplicity, often become most perfect therein. The Spirit of God needs none of our arrangements and methods; when it pleaseth him, he turns shepherds into prophets: and, so far from excluding any from the Temple of Prayer, he throws wide the gates, that all may enter; while Wisdom cries aloud in the highways, "Whoso is simple let him turn in hither" (Prov. 9:4); and to the Fools she saith, "Come eat of my bread, and drink of the wine which I have mingled" (Prov. 9:5). And doth not Jesus Christ himself thank his Father for having hid the secrets of his kingdom from the wise and prudent and revealed them unto babes? (Matt. 11:25).

CHAPTER 24

Of the Way to Attain Divine Union

It is impossible to attain Divine Union solely by the activity of meditation, or by the meltings of the affections, or even by the highest degree of luminous and distinctly-comprehended prayer. There are many reasons for this, the chief of which are as follows.

First, according to Scripture "no man shall see God and live" (Exod. 33:20). Now all the exercises of discursive prayer, and even of active contemplation (while esteemed as the summit and end of the passive, and not merely as a preparative to it), are still living exercises by which we cannot see God; that is to say, be united with him. For all that is of man's own power or exertion must first die, be it ever so noble, ever so exalted.

S. John relates "That there was a great silence in heaven" (Rev. 8:1). Now heaven represents the foundation and center of the soul, wherein, ere the Majesty of God appears, all must be hushed to silence. All the efforts, nay, the very existence of self-sufficiency must be destroyed, because nothing is opposite to God but self-sufficiency; and all the malignity of man is in this failing, as in the power of its evil nature, insomuch that the purity of a soul increases in proportion as it loses this quality; till at length that which had been a fault, while the soul lived in self-sufficiency and so acted, becomes no longer such, from the purity and innocence it hath acquired by departing from that which caused the dissimilitude between it and God.

Secondly, to unite two things so opposite, as the impurity of the creature and the purity of God; the simplicity of God and the multiplicity of man; much more is requisite than the impotent efforts of the creature. No less than a singular and efficacious operation of the Almighty can ever accomplish this, for things must be reduced to some familiarity before they can blend and become one. Can the impurity of dross be united with the purity of gold? What then does God do? He sends his own Wisdom before him, as the last fire shall be sent upon earth to destroy by its activity all that is impure therein; and as nothing can resist the power of that fire, in like manner this Wisdom dissolves and destroys all the impurities of the creature and disposes it for Divine Union.

This impurity, so opposite to Union, consists in self-sufficiency and activity.

This is the source and fountain of all that defilement and corruption which can never be allied to Essential Purity; the rays of the sun may glance, indeed, upon filth and mire, but can never be united with them. Activity obstructs Union; for God (being an Infinite Stillness), the soul, in order to be united to him, must participate in this stillness, else the contrariety between stillness and activity would prevent assimilation.

Therefore, the soul can never arrive at Divine Union but by the repose or stillness of the will, nor can it ever become one with God but by being re-established in the purity of its first creation, that is, in this central repose.

God purifies the soul by his Wisdom, as refiners do metals in the furnace. Gold cannot be purified but by fire, which gradually separates from and consumes all that is earthy and heterogeneous: it must be melted and dissolved, and all impure mixtures taken away by casting it again and again into the furnace; thus it is refined from all internal corruption, and even exalted to a state incapable of farther purification.

The goldsmith now no longer discovers any adulterate mixture; its purity is perfect, its simplicity complete. The fire no longer touches it; and were it to remain an age in the furnace its purity would not be increased nor its substance diminished. Then is it fit for the most exquisite workmanship: and if thereafter this gold seems obscured or defiled, it is no more than an accidental defilement contracted by its contiguity to some impure body; but this is only superficial, and widely different from its former impurity, which was hidden in the very center and ground of its nature and, as it were, identified with it. Those, however, who are ignorant of this process and its blessed effects would be apt to despise and reject the vessel of pure gold sullied by some external pollution, and prefer an impure and gross metal that appeared superficially bright and polished.

Farther, the goldsmith never mingles together the pure and the impure gold, lest the dross of the one should corrupt the other; before they can be united they must first be equally refined; he therefore plunges the impure metal into the furnace till all its dross is purged away and it becomes fully prepared for incorporation and union with the pure gold.

This is what S. Paul means when he declares that "the fire shall try every man's work of what sort [of work] it is" (1 Cor. 3:13). He adds, "If any man's work be burnt, he shall suffer loss; yet he himself shall be saved, yet so as by fire" (verse 15). He here intimates that there is a species of works so degraded by impure mixtures that though the mercy of God accepts them, yet they must pass through the fire to be purged from the contamination of Self; and it is in this sense that God is said to "examine and judge our righteousness" (Ps. 14:3), because that, "by the deeds of the law, there shall no flesh be justified, but by the righteousness of God, which is by faith in Jesus Christ" (Rom. 3:20, etc.).

Thus we see that the Divine Justice and Wisdom, as an unremitting fire, must devour and destroy all that is earthly, sensual, and carnal, and all self-activity, before the soul can be fitted for and capable of Union with God. Now this purification can never be accomplished by the industry of fallen man; on the contrary, he submits to it always with reluctance: he is so enamored of self, and so averse to its destruction, that did not God act upon him powerfully and with authority, he would forever resist.

It may, perhaps, be objected here that, as God never robs man of his free will, he can always resist the Divine Operations, and that I therefore err in saying God acts thus absolutely and without the consent of man.

Let me, however, explain myself. By man's giving a passive consent, God, without usurpation, may assume full power and entire guidance; for having in the beginning of his conversion, made an unreserved surrender of himself to all that God wills of him or by him, he thereby gave an active consent to whatsoever God thereafter might operate or require. But when God begins to burn, destroy, and purify, then the soul, not perceiving the salutary design of these operations, shrinks from them: and as the gold seems rather to blacken than brighten when first put into the furnace, so it conceives that its purity is lost and that its temptations are sins; insomuch that if an active and explicit consent were then requisite the soul could scarcely give it, nay, often would withhold it. The utmost the soul can do is to remain firm in a passive disposition, enduring as well as it is able all these Divine Operations, which it neither can, nor will, obstruct.

In this manner, therefore, the soul is purified from all proper, distinct, perceptible, and multiplied operations which constitute the great dissimilitude between it and God: it is rendered, by degrees, conformed, and then uniform; and the passive capacity of the creature is elevated, ennobled, and enlarged, though in a secret and hidden manner, and therefore called mystical: but in all these operations the soul must concur passively. It is true, indeed, that at the beginning of its purification activity is requisite; which as the Divine Operations become stronger and stronger it must gradually cease, yielding itself up to the impulses of the Divine Spirit, till wholly absorbed in him. But this is often a difficult and tedious process.

We do not then say, as some have falsely supposed, that there is no need for action in the process of Divine Purification; on the contrary, we affirm it is the gate; at which, however, we would not have those stop who are to obtain ultimate perfection, which is impracticable, except the first helps are laid aside. For, however necessary they may have been at the entrance of the road, they become afterwards mere clogs, and greatly detrimental to those who adhere to them, preventing them from ever arriving at the end of their course. This made S. Paul say, "Forgetting those things which are behind and reaching forth to those which are before, I press toward the mark for the prize of the high calling in Christ Jesus" (Phil. 3:13).

Would you not say that he had lost his senses, who, having undertaken an important journey, should fix his abode at the first inn because he had been told that many travelers who had come that way had lodged in the house and made it their place of residence? All that we would wish then is, that souls should press toward the mark, should pursue their journey, and take the shortest and easiest road; not stopping at the first stage, but following the counsel and example of S. Paul, suffer themselves to be guided and governed by the Spirit of Grace, which would infallibly conduct them to the end of their creation, the enjoyment of God. But, while we confess that the enjoyment of God is the end for which alone we were created; that without holiness none can attain it: and that to attain it, we must necessarily pass through a severe and purifying process—how strange is it that we should dread and avoid this process, as if that could be the cause of evil or imperfection in the present life, which is to be productive of glory and blessedness in the life to come!

None can be ignorant that God is the Supreme Good; that essential blessedness consists in Union with him; that the Saints are more or less glorified, according as this Union is more or less advanced; and that the soul cannot attain this Union by the mere activity of its own powers. For God communicates himself to the soul in proportion as its passive capacity is great, noble, and extensive. It cannot be united to God but in simplicity and passivity; and as this Union is beatitude itself, the way to it in simplicity and passivity, instead of being evil, must be good, must be most free from delusion and danger, the safest, the surest, and the best.

Would Jesus Christ have made this the most perfect and necessary way had there been evil or danger therein? No! All can travel this road to blessedness; and all are called thereto, as to the enjoyment of God, which alone is beatitude, both in this world and the next. I say the enjoyment of God himself, and not his gifts, which, as they do not constitute essential beatitude, cannot fully content an immortal spirit: the soul is so noble, so great, that the most exalted gifts of God cannot fill its immense capacity with happiness unless the Giver also bestows himself. Now the whole desire of the Divine Being is to give himself to every creature, according to the capacity with which it is endued; and yet, alas! How reluctantly man suffers himself to be drawn to God! How fearful is he to prepare for Divine Union!

Some say that we should not attempt, by our own ability, to place ourselves in this state. I grant it: but what a poor subterfuge is this? Since I

71

have all along asserted and proved that the utmost exertion of the highest created being could never accomplish this of itself: it is God alone must do it. The creature may, indeed, open the window; but it is the sun Himself that must give the light.

The same persons say again that some may feign to have attained this blessed state: but, alas! none can any more feign this than the wretch, who is on the point of perishing with hunger, can for a length of time, feign to be full and satisfied; some wish or word, some sigh or sign, will inevitably escape him, and betray his famished state.

Since then none can attain this blessed state save those whom God himself leads and places therein, we do not pretend to introduce any into it, but only to point out the shortest and safest road that leads to it: beseeching you not to be retarded in your progress by any external exercises, not to sit down a resident at the first inn, nor to be satisfied with the sweets which are tasted in the milk for babes. If the Water of Eternal Life is shown to some thirsty souls, how inexpressibly cruel would it be, by confining them to a round of external forms, to prevent their approaching it, so that their longing shall never be satisfied, but they shall perish with thirst!

Let us all agree in the way, as we all agree in the end, which is evident and incontrovertible. The way has its beginning, progress, and end; and the nearer we approach the end, the farther is the beginning behind us: it is only by proceeding from one that we can ever arrive at the other. Would you get from the entrance to the distant end of the road without passing over the intermediate space? And surely, if the end is good, holy, and necessary, and the entrance also good, can that be condemnable, as evil, which is the necessary passage, the direct road leading from the one to the other?

O ye blind and foolish men, who pride yourselves on science, wisdom, wit, and power, how well do you verify what God hath said, that "his secrets are hidden from the great and wise, and revealed unto the little ones—the babes!"[1]

---

[1] Luke 10:21: "In that hour Jesus rejoiced in spirit, and said, 'I thank thee, O Father, Lord of heaven and earth, that thou hast hid these things from the wise and prudent, and hast revealed them unto babes: even so, Father; for so it seemed good in thy sight.'" (KJV)

Spiritual Torrents

Introduction

to Allenson 1908 Edition

An experiment was recently made by the publishers of this reissue of Madame Guyon's *Spiritual Torrents* to reintroduce her and her works to English readers.[1] It is gratifying already to be able to state that *The Life, Experiences, etc., of Madame Guyon,* by Thomas Upham, has passed into its second edition, and that her precious little treatise, *A Short and Easy Method of Prayer,* has also passed beyond the experimental stage and found great favor with many readers. The present reissue of Miss Marston's translation is entered upon in similar trust, in response to many applications for its renewed appearance.

Of the experience of Madame Guyon, it should be borne in mind, that though the glorious heights of communion with God to which she attained may be scaled by the feeblest of God's chosen ones, yet it is by no

---

[1] The editor who wrote this introduction clearly was familiar with Madame Guyon. This version of *Spiritual Torrents* was published in 1908 by H.R. Allenson, London, having been translated by A.W. Marston from the 1790 Paris edition of the book. Shortly before this introduction was written, Allenson also published Guyon's official biography (Upham: *The Life of Madame Guyon,* 1905) and *A Short and Easy Method of Prayer* (1907).

means necessary that they should be reached by the same apparently arduous and protracted path along which she was led.

The *Torrents* especially needs to be regarded rather as an account of the personal experience of the author, than as the plan which God invariably, or even usually, adopts in bringing the soul into a state of union with himself. It is true that, in order that we may "live unto righteousness," we must be "dead indeed unto sin"; and that there must be a crucifixion of self before the life of Christ can be made manifest in us. It is only when we can say, "I am crucified with Christ," that we are able to add, "Nevertheless I live, yet not I, but Christ liveth in me." But it does not follow that this inward death must always be as lingering as in the case of Madame Guyon. She tells us herself that the reason was, that she was not wholly resigned to the Divine will, and willing to be deprived of the gifts of God, that she might enjoy the possession of the Giver. This resistance to the will of God implies suffering on the part of the creature, and chastisement on the part of God, in order that he may subdue to himself what is not voluntarily yielded to him.

Of the joy of a complete surrender to God, it is not necessary to speak here: thousands of God's children are realizing its blessedness for themselves, and proving that it is no hardship, but a joy unspeakable, to present themselves a living sacrifice to God, to live no longer to themselves, but to him that died for them, and rose again.

A simple trust in a living, personal Savior; a putting away by his grace of all that is known to be in opposition to his will; and an entire self-abandonment to him, that his designs may be worked out in and through us; such is the simple key to the hidden sanctuary of communion.

PART I

CHAPTER I

The Different Ways in Which Souls Are Led to Seek After God

Souls under divine influence are impelled to seek after God, but in different ways—reduced to three, and explained by a similitude.

As soon as a soul is brought under divine influence, and its return to God is true and sincere, after the first cleansing which Confession and contrition have effected, God imparts to it a certain instinct to return to him in a most complete manner, and to become united to him. The soul feels then that it was not created for the amusements and trifles of the world, but that it has a center and an end, to which it must be its aim to return, and out of which it can never find true repose.

This instinct is very deeply implanted in the soul, more or less in different cases, according to the designs of God; but all have a loving impatience to purify themselves, and to adopt the necessary ways and means of returning to their source and origin, like rivers, which, after leaving their source, flow on continuously, in order to precipitate themselves into the sea.

You will observe that some rivers move gravely and slowly, and others with greater velocity; but there are rivers and *torrents which* rush with frightful impetuosity, and which nothing can arrest. All the burdens which might be laid upon them, and the obstructions which might be placed to impede their course, would only serve to redouble their violence. It is thus with souls. Some go on quietly towards perfection, and never reach the sea, or only very late, contented to lose themselves in some stronger and more rapid river, which carries them with itself into the sea.

Others, which form the second class, flow on more vigorously, and promptly than the first. They even carry with them a number of rivulets; but they are slow and idle in comparison with the last class, which rush onward with so much impetuosity, that they are utterly useless: they are not available for navigation, nor can any merchandise be trusted upon them, except at certain parts and at certain times. These are bold and mad rivers, which dash against the rocks, which terrify by their noise, and which stop at nothing. The second class are more agreeable and more useful; their gravity is pleasing, they are all laden with merchandise, and we sail upon them without fear or peril.

Let us look, with divine aid, at these three classes of persons, under the three figures that I have proposed; and we will commence with the first, in order to conclude happily with the last.

Chapter 2

Of the First Way, Which Is Active and Meditative

Of the first way, which is active, and of meditation—What it is—Its weaknesses, habits, occupations, advantages, etc.—General opinion—Want of observation the cause of most of the disputes and difficulties which have arisen upon the passive way, and the absurd objections which have been made to it—Souls for meditation—they should be led to it through the affections—Opinion concerning their barrenness and powerlessness—Spiritual books and authors on the inner life, in contrast to others—Capacity and incapacity of souls—the simple are better than the great reasoners.

The first class of souls are those who, after their conversion, give themselves up to meditation, or even to works of charity. They perform some exterior austerities; endeavor, little by little, to purify themselves, to rid themselves of certain notable sins, and even of voluntary venial ones. They endeavor, with all their little strength, to advance gradually, but it is feebly and slowly.

As their source is not abundant, the dryness sometimes causes delay. There are even periods, in times of aridity, when they dry up altogether. They do not cease to flow from the source, but it is so feebly as to be barely perceptible. These rivers carry little or no merchandise, and, therefore, for the public need, it must be taken to them. It is necessary, at the same time, that art should assist nature, and find the means of enlarging them, either by canals, or by the help of other rivers of the same kind, which are joined together and united to it, which rivers thus joined increase the body of water, and, helping each other, put themselves in a condition to carry a few small boats, not to the sea, but to some of the chief rivers, of which we shall speak later. Such beings have usually little depth of spiritual life. They work outwardly, and rarely quit their meditations, so that they are not fit for great things. In general they carry no merchandise—that is to say, they can impart nothing to others; and God seldom uses them, unless it be to carry a few little boats—that is, to minister to bodily necessities; and in order to be used, they must be discharged into the canals of sensible graces, or united to some others in religion, by which means several, of medium grace, manage to carry the small boat, but not into the sea itself, which is God: into that they never enter in this life, but only in the next.

It is not that souls are not sanctified in this way. There are many people, who pass for being very virtuous, who never get beyond it, God giving them lights conformed to their condition, which are sometimes very beautiful, and are the admiration of the religious world. The most highly favored of this class are diligent in the practice of virtue. They devise thousands of holy inventions and practices to lead them to God, and to enable them to abide in his presence; but all is accomplished by their own efforts, aided and supported by grace, and their own works appear to exceed the work of God, his work only concurring with theirs.

The spiritual life of this class only thrives in proportion to their work. If this work be removed, the progress of grace within them is arrested: they resemble pumps, which only yield water in proportion as they are agitated. You will observe in them a great tendency to assist themselves by means of their natural sensibilities, a vigorous activity, a desire to be always doing something more and something new to promote their perfection, and, in their seasons of barrenness, an anxiety to rid themselves of it. They are subject to great variation: sometimes they do wonders, at other times they languish and decline. They have no evenness of conduct, because, as the greater part of their religion is in these natural sensibilities, whenever it happens that their sensibilities are dry, either from want of work on their part, or from a lack of correspondence on the part of God, they fall into discouragement, or else they redouble their efforts, in the hope of recovering of themselves what they have lost. They never possess, like others, a profound peace or calmness in the midst of distractions; on the contrary, they are always on the alert to struggle against them or to complain of them.

Such minds must not be directed to passive devotion; this would be to ruin them irrecoverably, taking from them their means of access to God. For as with a person who is compelled to travel, and who has neither boat nor carriage, nor any other alternative than that of going on foot, if you remove his feet, you place advancement beyond his reach; so with these souls; if you take away their works, which are their feet, they can never advance.

And I believe this to be the cause of the contests which now agitate the religious world. Those who are in the *passive* way, conscious of the blessedness they experience in it, would compel all to walk with them; those, on the contrary, who are in what I have termed the state of *meditation*, would confine all to their way, which would involve inestimable loss.

What must be done then? We must take the middle course, and see for which of the two ways souls are fitted.

This may be known in some by the opposition they have to remaining at rest, and allowing themselves to be led by the Spirit of God; by a confusion of faults and defects into which they fall without being conscious of them; or, if they are possessed of natural prudence, by a certain skill in concealing their faults from others and from themselves; by their adherence to their sentiments, and by a number of other indications which cannot be explained.

The way to deliver them from such a state would be, to lead them to live less in the intellect and more in the affections, and if it be manifest that they are gradually substituting the one for the other, it is a sign that a spiritual work is being carried on within them.

I am at a loss to understand why so loud a cry is raised against those books and writers that treat [deal with] the inner life. I maintain that they can do no harm, unless it be to some who are willing to lose themselves for the sake of their own pleasure, to whom not only these things, but everything else, would be an injury like spiders, which convert flowers into venom. But they can do no injury to those humble souls who are desirous for perfection, because it is impossible for any to understand them to whom the special light is not accorded; and whatever others may read, they cannot rightly understand those conditions which, being beyond the range of imagination, can be known only by experience. Perfection goes on with a steady advancement corresponding to the progress of the inner life.

Not that there are no persons advanced in sanctification who have faults in appearance even greater than those of others, but they are not the same either as to their nature or their quality.

The second reason why I say that such books can do no harm is, that they demand so much natural death, so much breaking off, so many things to be conquered and destroyed, that no one would ever have strength for the undertaking without sincerity of purpose; or even if anyone undertook it, it would only produce the effect of *meditation*, which is to endeavor to destroy itself.

As for those who wish to lead others in their groove, and not in God's, and to place limits to their further advancement—as for those, I say, who know but one way, and would have all the world to walk in it—the evils which they bring upon others are irremediable, for they keep them all their lives stopping at certain things which hinder God from blessing them infinitely.

It seems to me that we must act in the divine life as in a school. The scholars are not kept always in the same class, but are passed on to others more advanced. O human science! You are so little worth, and yet with you men do not fail to take every precaution! O science mysterious and divine! You are so great and so necessary; and yet they neglect you, they limit you, they contract you, they do violence to you! Oh, will there never be a school of religion! Alas! By wishing to make it a study, man has marred it. He has sought to give rules and limits to the Spirit of God, who is without limit.

O poor powerless souls! You are better fitted to answer God's purposes, and, if you are faithful, your devotion will be more pleasing to him, than that of those great intellects which make prayer a study rather than a devotion. More than this, I say that such souls as these, who appear so powerless and so incapable, are worthy of consideration, provided they only knock at the door, and wait with a humble patience until it be opened to them. Those persons of great intellect and subtle understanding—who cannot remain a moment in silence before God, who make a continual Babel, who are so well able to give an account of their devotion in all its parts, who go through it always according to their own will, and with the same method, who exercise themselves as they will on any subject which suggests itself to them, who are so well satisfied with themselves and their light, who expatiate upon the preparation and the methods for prayer—will make but little advance in it; and after ten or twenty years of this exercise, will always remain the same.

Alas! When it is a question of loving a miserable creature, do they use a method for that? The most ignorant in such a matter are the most skillful. It is the same, and yet very different, with divine love. Therefore, if one who has never known such religion comes to you to learn it, teach him to love God much, and to let himself go with a perfect abandonment into love, and he will soon know it. If it be a nature slow to love, let him do his best, and wait in patience till love itself make itself beloved in its own way, and not in yours.

CHAPTER 3

Of the Second Way, Which Is the Passive Way of Light

Of the second way of the return of the soul to God, which is the passive way, but one of light, and of two kinds of introduction to it—Description of this class, and of its striking advantages—Various necessary precautions and observations concerning this class, their conduct, perfections, imperfections, and experiences.

The second class are like those large rivers which move with a slow and steady course. They flow with pomp and majesty; their course is direct and easily followed; they are charged with merchandise, and can go on to the sea without mingling with other rivers; but they are late in reaching it, being grave and slow. There are even some who never reach it at all, and these, for the most part, lose themselves in other larger rivers, or else turn aside to some arm of the sea. Many of these rivers serve to carry merchandise, and are heavily laden with it. They may be kept back by sluices, and turned off at certain points. Such are the souls in the *passive way of sight*. Their strength is very abundant; they are laden with gifts, and graces, and celestial favors; they are the admiration of their generation and numbers of saints who shine as stars in the Church have never passed this limit. This class is composed of two kinds. The first commenced in the ordinary way, and have afterwards been drawn to passive contemplation. The others have been, as it were, taken by surprise; they have been seized by the heart, and they feel themselves loving without having learned to know the object of their love.

For there is this difference between divine and human love, that the latter supposes a previous acquaintance with its object, because, as it is outside of it, the senses must be taken to it, and the senses can only be taken to it because it is communicated to them: the eyes see and the heart loves. It is not so with divine love. God, having an absolute power over the heart of man, and being its origin and its end; it is not necessary that he should make known to it what he is. He takes it by assault, without giving it battle. The heart is powerless to resist him, even though he may not use an absolute and violent authority, unless it be in some cases where he permits it to be so, in order to manifest his power. He takes hearts, then, in this way, making them burn in a moment; but usually he gives them flashes of light which dazzle them, and lift them nearer to himself. These persons appear much greater than those of whom I shall speak later, to those who are not possessed of a divine discernment, for they attain outwardly to a high degree of perfection, God eminently elevating their natural capacity, and replenishing it in an extraordinary manner; and yet they are never really brought to a state of annihilation to self, and God does not usually so draw them out of their own being that they become lost in Himself. Such characters as these are, however, the wonder and admiration of men. God bestows on them gifts upon gifts, graces upon graces, visions, revelations, inward voices, ecstasies, ravishments, etc. It seems as though God's only care was to enrich and beautify them, and to communicate to them his secrets. All joys are theirs.

This does not imply that they bear no heavy crosses, no fierce temptations: these are the shadows which cause their virtues to shine with greater brilliancy; for these temptations are thrust back vigorously, the crosses are borne bravely; they even desire more of them: they are all flame and fire, enthusiasm and love. God uses them to accomplish great things, and it seems as though they only need to desire a thing in order to receive it from God, he finding his delight in satisfying all their desires and doing all their will. Yet in the same path there are various degrees of progression, and some attain a far higher standard of perfection than others; their danger lies in fixing their thoughts upon what God has done for them, thus stopping at the gifts, instead of being led *through them* to the Giver.

The design of God in the bestowal of his grace, and in the profusion with which he gives it, is to bring them nearer to himself; but they make use of it for an utterly different end: they rest in it, reflect upon it, look at it, and appropriate it; and hence arise vanity, complaisance,[1] self esteem, the preference of themselves to others, and often the destruction of religious life. These people are admirable, in themselves considered; and sometimes by a special grace they are made very helpful to others, particularly if they have been brought from great depths of sin. But usually they are less fitted to lead others than those who come after; for being near to God themselves, they have a horror of sin, and often a shrinking from sinners, and never having experienced the miseries they see in others, they are astonished, and unable to render either help or advice. They expect too great perfection, and do not lead on to it little by little, and if they meet with weak ones, they do not aid them in proportion to their own advancement, or in accordance with God's designs, but often even seek to avoid them. They find it difficult to converse with those who have not reached their own level, preferring a solitary life to all the ministry of love.

If such persons were heard in conversation by those not divinely enlightened, they would be believed equal to the last class, or even more advanced. They make use of the same terms—of *death, loss of self, annihilation,* etc.; and it is quite true that they do die in their own way, that they are annihilated and lose themselves, for often their natural sensibilities are lost or suspended in their seasons of devotion; they even lose the habit of making use of them. Thus these souls are passive, but they have light, and love, and strength in themselves; they like to retain something of their own, it may be even their virtues, but in so delicate a form that only the Divine eye can detect it. Such as these are so laden with merchandise that their course is very slow. What must be done with them, then, to lead them out of this way? There is a more safe and certain path for them, even that of faith: they need to be led from

---

[1] Complaisance: the inclination to comply willingly with the wishes of others. (*American Heritage Dictionary,* 2000.)

the sensible to the supernatural, from that which is known and perceived to the very deep, yet very safe, darkness of faith. It is useless to endeavor to ascertain whether these things be of God or not, since they must be surpassed; for if they are of God, they will be carried on by him, if only we abandon ourselves to him; and if they are not of God, we shall not be deceived by them, if we do not stay at them.

This class of people find far greater difficulty in entering the way of faith than the first, for as what they already possess is so great, and so evidently from God, they will not believe that there is anything higher in the Church of God. Therefore they cling to it.

O God! How many spiritual possessions there are which appear great virtues to those who are not divinely enlightened, and which appear great and dangerous defects to those who are so! For those in this way regard as virtues what others look upon as subtle faults; and even the light to see them in their true colors is not given to them. These people have rules and regulations for their obedience, which are marked by prudence; they are strong and vigorous, though they appear dead. They are indeed dead as to their own wants, but not as to their foundation. Such souls as these often possess an inner silence, certain sinkings into God, which they distinguish and express well; but they have not that secret longing to be *nothing*, like the last class. It is true they desire to be nothing by a certain perceptible annihilation, a deep humility, an abasement under the immense weight of God's greatness. All this is an annihilation in which they dwell without being annihilated. They have the feeling of annihilation without the reality, for the soul is still sustained by its feelings, and this state is more satisfactory to it than any other, for it gives more assurance. This class usually are only brought into God by death, unless it be some privileged ones, whom God designs to be the lights of his Church, or whom he designs to sanctify more eminently; and such he robs by degrees of all their riches. But as there are few sufficiently courageous to be willing, after so much blessedness, to lose it all: few pass this point, God's intention perhaps being that they should not pass it, and that, as in the Father's house there are many mansions, they should only occupy this one. Let us leave the causes with God.

CHAPTER 4

*Of the Third Way, Which Is the Passive Way of Faith,
and of Its First Degree*

*Of the third way of return to God, which is the passive way of faith, and of
its first degree—Description of this way under the similitude of a torrent—Propensity of the soul towards God—Its properties, obstacles, and
effects explained by the similitude of fire—What befalls the soul called to
walk in the passive way of faith—Description of the first degree of this third
way, and of the state of the soul in it—The rest it finds in it would be hurtful if God did not draw it out of it, in order to further its advancement.*

What shall we say of the souls in this *third way*, unless it be that they
resemble *torrents* which rise in high mountains? They have their source in
God himself, and they have not a moment's rest until they are lost in him.
Nothing stops them, and no burdens are laid upon them. They rush on
with a rapidity that alarms even the most confident. These torrents flow
without order, here and there, wherever they can find a passage, having
neither regular beds nor an orderly course. They sometimes become

muddy by passing through ground which is not firm, and which they bear away with them by their rapidity. Sometimes they appear to be irrecoverably lost, then they reappear for a time, but it is only to precipitate themselves in another abyss, still deeper than the former one. It is the sport of these torrents to show themselves, to lose themselves, and to break themselves upon the rocks. Their course is so rapid as to be indiscernible; but finally, after many precipices and abysses, after having been dashed against rocks, and many times lost and found again, they reach the sea, where they are lost, to be found no more. And there, however poor, mean, useless, destitute of merchandise the poor torrent may have been, it is wonderfully enriched, for it is not rich with its own riches, like other rivers, which only bear a certain amount of merchandise or certain rarities, but it is rich with the riches of the sea itself. It bears on its bosom the largest vessels; it is the sea which bears them, and yet it is the river, because the river, being lost in the sea, has become one with it.

It is to be remarked, that the river or torrent thus precipitated into the sea does not lose its nature, although it is so changed and lost as not to be recognized. It will always remain what it was, yet its identity is lost, not as to reality, but as to quality; for it so takes the properties of salt water, that it has nothing peculiar to itself, and the more it loses itself and remains in the sea, the more it exchanges its own nature for that of the sea. For what, then, is not this poor torrent fitted? Its capacity is unlimited, since it is the same as that of the sea; it is capable of enriching the whole earth. O happy loss! Who can set thee forth? Who can describe the gain which has been made by this useless and good-for-nothing river, despised and looked upon as a mad thing, on which the smallest boat could not be trusted, because, not being able to restrain itself, it would have dragged the boat with it. What do you say of the fate of this torrent, O great rivers! which flow with such majesty, which are the delight and admiration of the world, and glory in the quantity of merchandise spread out upon you? The fate of this poor torrent, which you regard with contempt, or at best with compassion, what has it become? What use can it serve now, or rather, what use can it *not* serve? What does it lack? You are now its servants, since the riches which you possess are only the overflow of its abundance, or a fresh supply which you are carrying to it.

But before speaking of the happiness of a soul thus lost in God, we must begin with its origin and go on by degrees.

The soul, as we have said, having proceeded from God, has a continual propensity to return to him, because, as he is its origin, he is also its final end. Its course would be interminable if it were not arrested or interrupted by sin and unbelief. Therefore the heart of man is perpetually in motion, and can find no rest till it returns to its origin and its center, which is God: like fire, which, being removed from its sphere, is in continual agitation, and does not rest till it has returned to it, and then, by a miracle of nature, this element, so active itself as to consume everything by its activity, is at perfect rest. O poor soul who is seeking happiness in this life! You will never find it out[side] of God. Seek to return to him: there all your longings and troubles, your agitations and anxieties, will be reduced to perfect rest.

It is to be remarked, that in proportion as fire approaches its center, it always approaches rest, although its swiftness increases. It is the same with the soul: as soon as sin ceases to hold it back, it seeks indefatigably to find God; and if it were not for sin, nothing could impede its course, which would be so speedy, that it would soon attain its end. But it is also true that, in proportion as it approaches God, its speed is augmented, and at the same time becomes more peaceful; for the rest, or rather the peace (since it is not at rest, but is pursuing a peaceful course), increases so that its peace redoubles its speed, and its speed increases its peace.

The hindrances, then, arise from sins and imperfections, which arrest for a time the course of the soul, more or less, according to the magnitude of the fault. Then the soul is conscious of its activity, as though when fire was going on towards its center, it encountered obstacles, such as pieces of wood or straw: it would resume its former activity in order to consume these obstacles or barriers, and the greater the obstacle the more its activity would increase. If it were a piece of wood, a longer and stronger activity would be needed to consume it; but if it were only a straw, it would be burned up in a moment, and would but very slightly impede its course. You will notice that the obstacles which the fire would encounter would only impart to it a fresh stimulus to surmount all which prevented its union with its center; again, it is to be remarked, that the more obstacles the fire might encounter, and the more considerable they might be, the more they would retard its course; and if it were continually meeting with fresh ones, it would be kept back, and prevented from returning whence it came.

We know by experience, that if we continually add fuel to fire, we shall keep it down, and prevent its rising. It is the same with the souls of men. Their instincts and natural propensities lead them towards God. They would advance incessantly, were it not for the hindrances they meet. These hindrances are sins and imperfections, which prove the greater obstacles in the way of their return to God, according as they are serious and lasting; so that if they continue in sin, they will never reach their end. Those, therefore, who have not sinned so grossly as others, should [in theory] advance much more rapidly. This usually is the case, and yet it seems as though God took pleasure in making "grace abound where sin has most abounded" (Rom. 5:20).

I believe that one of the reasons of this, to be found in those who have not grossly sinned, is their estimation of their own righteousness, and this is an obstacle more difficult to surmount then even the grossest sins, because we cannot have so great an attachment to sins which are so hideous in themselves, as we have to our own righteousness; and God, who will not do violence to liberty, leaves such hearts to enjoy their holiness at their own pleasure, while he finds his delight in purifying the most miserable. And in order to accomplish his purpose, he sends a stronger and fiercer fire, which consumes those gross sins more easily than a slower fire consumes smaller obstacles. It even seems as though God loved to set up his throne in these criminal hearts, in order to manifest his power, and to show how he can restore the disfigured soul to its original condition, and even make it more beautiful than it was before it fell. Those then who have greatly sinned, and for whom I now write, are conscious of a great fire consuming all their sins and hindrances; they often find their course impeded by besetting sins, but this fire consumes them again and again, till they are completely subdued. And as the fire thus goes on consuming, the obstacles are more and more easily surmounted, so that at last they are no more than straws, which, far from impeding its course, only make it burn the more fiercely.

Let us then take the soul in its original condition, and follow it through its various stages, if God (who inspires these thoughts, which only occur to me as I write), wills that we should do so.

As God's design for the soul is that it should be lost in himself, in a manner unknown to ordinary Christians, he begins his work by imparting to it a sense of its distance from him. As soon as it has perceived and felt this distance, the natural inclination which it has to return to its source, and which has been, as it were, deadened by sin, is revived. Then the soul experiences true sorrow for sin, and is painfully conscious of the evil which is caused by this separation from God. This sentiment thus implanted in the soul leads it to seek the means of ridding itself of this trouble, and of entering into a certain rest which it sees from afar, but which only redoubles its anxiety, and increases its desire to pursue it until it finds it.

Some of those who are thus exercised, having never been taught that they must seek to have God within them, and not expect to find him in outward righteousness, give themselves up to meditation, and seek without what can only be found within. This meditation (in which they seldom succeed, because God, who has better things in store for them, does not permit them to find any rest in such an experience), only serves to increase their longing; for their wound is at the heart, and they apply the plaster externally, which does but foster the disease, instead of healing it. They struggle a long time with this exercise, and their struggling does but increase their powerlessness; and unless God, who himself assumes the charge of them, sends some messenger to show them a different way, they will lose their time, and will lose it just so long as they remain unaided.

But God, who is abundant in goodness, does not fail to send them help, though it may be but passing and temporary. As soon, then, as they are taught that they cannot advance because their wound is an internal one, and they are seeking to heal it by external applications; when they are led to seek in the depths of their own hearts what they have sought in vain out of themselves; then they find, with an astonishment which overwhelms them, that they have within them a treasure which they have been seeking far off. Then they rejoice in their new liberty; they marvel that prayer is no longer a burden, and that the more they retire within themselves, the more they taste of a certain mysterious something which ravishes them and carries them away, and they would wish ever to love thus, and thus to be buried within themselves. Yet what they experience, delightful as it may appear, does not stop them, if they are to be led into pure faith, but leads them to follow after something more, which they have not yet known. They are now all ardor and love. They seem already to be in Paradise; for what they possess within themselves is infinitely sweeter than all the joys of earth: these they can leave without pain; they would leave the whole world to enjoy for one hour their present experience. They find that prayer has become their continual attitude; their love increases day by day, so that their one desire is always to love and never to be interrupted. And as they are not now strong enough to be undisturbed by conversation, they shun and fear it; they love to be alone, and to enjoy the caresses of their Beloved. They have within themselves a Counselor, who lets them find no pleasure in earthly things, and who does not suffer them to commit a single fault, without making them feel by His coldness how much sin is displeasing to Him. This coldness of God in times of transgression, is to them the most terrible chastisement. It seems as though God's only care were to correct and reprove them, and his one purpose to perfect them. It is a surprise to themselves and to others that they change more in a month by this way, and even in a day, than in several years by the other. O God! it belongs only to Thee to correct and to purify the hearts of thy children!

God has yet another means of chastising the soul, when it is further advanced in the divine life, by making himself more fully known to it after it falls. Then the poor soul is covered with confusion; it would rather bear the most severe chastisement than this goodness of God after it has sinned.

These persons are now so full of their own feelings that they want to impart them to others; they long to teach the whole world to love God; their sentiments towards him are so deep, so pure, and so disinterested, that those who hear them speak, if they are not divinely enlightened, believe them to have attained the height of perfection. They are fruitful in good works; there is no reasoning here, nothing but a deep and burning love. The soul feels itself seized and held fast by a divine force which ravishes and consumes it. It is like intoxicated persons, who are so possessed with wine that they do not know what they are doing, and are no longer masters of themselves. If such as these try to read, the book falls from their hands, and a single line suffices them; they can hardly get through a page in a whole day, however assiduously they may devote themselves to it, for a single word from God awakens that secret instinct which animates and fires them, so that love closes both their mouth and their eyes. They cannot utter verbal prayers, being unable to pronounce them. A heart which is unaccustomed to this does not know what it means; for it has never experienced anything like it before, and it does not understand why it cannot pray, and yet it cannot resist the power which overcomes it. It cannot be troubled, nor be fearful of doing wrong, for he [God] who holds it bound does not permit it either to doubt that it is he who thus holds it, or to strive against it, for if it makes an effort to pray, it feels that he who possesses it closes its lips, and compels it, by a sweet and loving violence, to be silent. Not that the creature cannot resist and speak by an effort, but besides doing violence to himself he loses this divine peace, and feels that he is becoming dry: he must allow himself to be moved upon by God at His will, and not in his own way. The soul in this state imagines itself to be in an inward silence, because its working is so gentle, so easy, and so quiet that it does not perceive it. It believes itself to have reached the summit of perfection, and it sees nothing before it but enjoyment of the wealth it possesses.

These Christians, so ardent and so desirous after God, begin to rest in their condition, and gradually and insensibly to lose the loving activity in seeking after God which formerly characterized them, being satisfied with their joy which they substituted for God himself; and this rest would be to them an irreparable loss, if God, in his infinite goodness, did not draw them out of this state to lead them into one more advanced. But before speaking of it, let us look at the imperfections of this stage.

CHAPTER 5

Imperfections of This First Degree

Imperfections, interior and exterior, of this first degree—Mistakes that are made in it—Its passivity—Spiritual dryness, mingled with a tender but self-interested love, which needs the experience and purifications of the following Degree.

The soul in the degree of which I have just spoken can and does make great advances, going from love to love, and from cross to cross; but it falls so frequently, and is so selfish, that it may be said to move only at a snail's pace, although it appears to itself and to others to progress infinitely. The torrent is now in a flat country, and has not yet found the slope of the mountain down which it may precipitate itself, and take a course which is never to be stopped.

The faults of those in this degree are a certain self esteem, more hidden and deeply rooted than it was before they had received these graces and favors from God; a certain secret contempt for others whom they see so far behind themselves, and a certain hardness for sin and sinners; a zeal

97

of St. John before the descent of the Holy Ghost, when he wanted to call down fire from heaven upon the Samaritans to consume them; a certain confidence in their own safety and virtue; a secret pride, which causes them to grieve specially over the faults which they commit in public. They appropriate the gifts of God, and treat them as though they were their own. They forget weakness and poverty in the strength which they possess, so that they lose all self-distrust. Though all this and much more is to be found in persons in this degree, they are themselves unconscious of it; but these faults will make themselves known in time. The grace which they feel so strongly in themselves being an assurance to them that they have nothing to fear, they allow themselves to speak without being divinely commissioned. They are anxious to communicate what they feel to everyone else.

It is true that they are of use to others, for their burning words take hold of the hearts of those who hear them; but apart from the fact that they cannot do the good they *would* do (if God would have them impart to others what they have received), they are giving out of their *necessity* and not of their *abundance*; so that they exhaust themselves; as you have seen in several pools of water under a fountain. The fountain alone gives out of its abundance, and the pools only send into each other of the fullness which is communicated to them; but if the fountain be closed or turned aside, and the pools cease to overflow, then as they are cut off from the source, they dry up. This is precisely what happens to those in this degree. They want to be constantly sending out their waters, and it is not till late that they perceive that the water which they had was only for themselves, and that they are not in a state to communicate it, because they are not connected with the source. They are like bottles of scent which are left open: they find so much sweetness in the odor which they emit that they do not perceive the loss they themselves sustain. Yet they appear to practice virtue without any effort, since they are occupied only with a general love, without reason or motive. If you ask them what they do during the day, they will tell you that they love; but if you ask why they love, they will tell you that they do not know; they only know that they love, and that they burn with desire to suffer for the object of their love. You may ask if it is not the sight of the sufferings of their Beloved which inspires them with the longing to suffer with him, but they will reply that the thought of his sufferings did not even enter their mind. Neither is it the desire to imitate the virtues which they see in him, for they do not think of them, nor the sight of his beauty which enraptures them, for they do not look at it. Only they feel in the depths of their heart a deep wound, yet so delightful that they rest in their pain, and find their pleasure in their grief.

They believe now that they have arrived at the consummation of all, for though they are full of the faults I have mentioned, and many others yet more dangerous, which are better perceived in the following degree than in this. They rest in their fancied perfection, and, stopping at the means, which they mistake for the end, they would remain stationary, if God did not bring the torrent, which is now like a peaceful lake on a mountain top, to the brow of the hill in order to precipitate it, and to start it on a course which will be more or less rapid according to the depth of its fall.

It appears to me that even the most advanced in this degree have a habit of concealing their faults, both from themselves and others, always finding excuses and extenuations; not designedly, but from a certain love of their own excellence, and a habitual dissimulation under which they hide themselves. The faults which cause them the deepest solicitude are those which are most apparent to others. They have a hidden love of self, stronger than ever, an esteem for their own position, a secret desire to attract attention, an affected modesty, a facility in judging others, and a preference for private devotion rather than domestic duties, which renders them the cause of many of the sins of those around them. This is of great importance. The soul, feeling itself drawn so strongly and sweetly, desires to be always alone and in prayer, which gives rise to two evils. The first: that in its seasons of greatest liberty it spends too much time in solitude. The second: that when its vigor of love is exhausted, as it often is in this way, it has not the same strength in times of dryness; it finds it difficult to remain so long in prayer; it readily shortens the time; its thoughts wander to exterior objects; then it is discouraged and cast down, thinking that all is lost, and does everything in its power to restore itself to the presence and favor of God.

But if such persons were strong enough to live an even life, and not to seek to do more in seasons of abundance than in times of barrenness, they would satisfy everyone. As it is, they are troublesome to those around them, to whom they cannot condescend, making it a favor to lay themselves out for the satisfaction of others: they preserve an austere silence when it is unnecessary, and at other times talk incessantly of the things of God. A wife has scruples about pleasing her husband, entertaining him, walking with him, or seeking to amuse him, but has none about speaking uselessly for two hours with religious devotees. This is a horrible abuse. We ought to be diligent in the discharge of all duties, whatever their nature may be; and even if they do cause us inconvenience, we shall yet find great profit in doing this, not perhaps in the way we imagine, but in hastening the crucifixion of self.

It even seems as though our Lord shows that such sacrifice is pleasing to him by the grace which he sheds upon it. I knew a lady who, when playing at cards with her husband in order to please him, experienced such deep and intimate communion with God as she never felt in prayer, and it was the same with everything she did at her husband's desire; but if she neglected these things for others which she thought better, she was conscious that she was not walking in the will of God. This did not prevent her often committing faults, because the attractions of meditation and the happiness of devotion (which are preferred to these apparent losses of time), insensibly draw the soul away, and lead it to change its course, and this by most people is looked upon as sanctity. However, those who are to be taught the way of faith are not suffered long to remain in these errors, because, as God designs to lead them on to better things, he makes them conscious of their deficiency.

It often happens, too, that persons by means of this death to self, and acting contrary to their natural inclinations, feel themselves more strongly drawn to their inward rest; for it is natural to man to desire most strongly what it is most difficult for him to obtain, and to desire most intensely those things which he most earnestly resolves to avoid. This difficulty of being able to enjoy only a partial rest increases the rest, and causes them even in activity to feel themselves acted upon so powerfully that they seem to have two souls within them, the inner one being infinitely stronger than the outer. But if they leave their duties in order to give the time to devotion, they will find it an empty form, and all its joy will be lost.

By devotion I do not mean compulsory prayer, which is gone through as a duty that must not be avoided; neither do I understand by activity the labors of their own choice, but those which come within the range of positive duty. If they have spare time at their disposal, by all means let them spend it in prayer; nor must they lay upon themselves unnecessary burdens, and call them obligations. When the taste for meditation is very great, the soul does not usually fall into these last named errors, but rather into the former one, that of courting retirement. I knew a person who spent more time in prayer when it was painful to her than when she felt it a delight, struggling with the disinclination. But this is injurious to the health, because of the violence which it does to the senses and the understanding, which (being unable to concentrate themselves upon any one object, and being deprived of the sweet communion which formerly held them in subjection to God), endure such torment, that the subject of it would rather suffer the greatest trial than the violence which is necessary to enable it to fix its thoughts on God. The person to whom I alluded sometimes passed two or three hours successively in this painful devotion, and she has assured me that the strangest austerities would have been delightful to her in comparison with the time thus spent. But as a violence so strong as this in subjects so weak is calculated to ruin both body and mind, I think it is better not in any way to regulate the time spent in prayer by our varying emotions.

This painful dryness of which I have spoken belongs only to the first degree of faith, and is often the effect of exhaustion; and yet those who have passed through it imagine themselves dead, and write and speak of it as the most sorrowful part of the spiritual life. It is true they have not known the contrary experience, and often they have not the courage to pass through this, for in this sorrow the soul is deserted by God, who withdraws from it his *sensible* helps. But it is nevertheless caused by the senses, because (being accustomed to see and to feel, and never having experienced a similar privation), they are in despair; which however is not of long duration, for the forces of the soul are not then in a state to bear for long such a pressure; it will either go back to seek for spiritual food, or else it will give all up. This is why the Lord does not fail to return: sometimes he does not even suffer the prayer to cease before he reappears; and if he does not return during the hour of prayer, he comes in a more manifest way during the day.

It seems as though he repented of the suffering he has caused to the soul of his beloved, or that he would pay back with usury what she has suffered for his love. If this consolation last for many days, it becomes painful. She calls him sweet and cruel: she asks him if he has only wounded her that she may die. But this kind Lover laughs at her pain, and applies to the wound a balm so sweet, that she could ask to be continually receiving fresh wounds, that she might always find a new delight in a healing which not only restores her former health, but imparts one yet more abundant.

Hitherto it has only been a play of love, to which the soul would easily become accustomed if her Beloved did not change his conduct. O poor hearts who complain of the flights of love! You do not know that this is only a farce, an attempt, a specimen of what is to follow. The hours of absence mark the days, the weeks, the months, and the years. You must learn to be generous at your own expense, to suffer your Beloved to come and go at his pleasure.

I seem to see these young brides. They are at the height of grief when their Beloved leaves them: they mourn his absence as if it were death, and endeavor, as far as they can, to prevent his departure. This love appears deep and strong, but it is not so by any means. It is the pleasure they derive from the sight of their Beloved which they mourn after. It is their own satisfaction they seek, for if it were the pleasure of their Beloved, they would rejoice in the pleasure which he found apart from them, as much as in that which he found with them. So it is self-interested love, though it does not appear such to them; on the contrary, they believe that they only love him for what he is. It is true, poor souls, you do love him for what he is, but you love him because of the pleasure you find in what he is. You reply that you are willing to suffer for your Beloved. True, provided he will be the witness and the companion of your suffering. You say you desire no recompense. I agree; but you do desire that he should know of your suffering, and approve of it. You want him to take pleasure in it. Is there anything more plausible than the desire that He for whom we suffer should know it, and approve of it, and take delight in it? Oh, how much you are out in your reckoning! Your jealous Lover will not permit you to enjoy the pleasure which you take in seeing his satisfaction with your sorrow. You must suffer without his appearing to see it, or to approve of it, or to know it. That would be too great a gratification. What pain would we not suffer on such conditions! What! To know that our Beloved sees our woes, and takes an infinite pleasure in them! This is too great a pleasure for a generous heart! Yet I am sure the greatest generosity of those in this Degree never goes beyond this. But to suffer without our Beloved being aware of it, when he seems to despise what we do to please him, and to turn away from it; to have only scorn for what formerly seemed to charm him; to see him repay with a terrible coldness and distance what we do for his sake alone, and with terrible flights all our pursuit of him; to lose without complaint all that he had formerly given as pledges of his love, and which we think we have repaid by our love, our fidelity, and our suffering; not only uncomplainingly to suffer ourselves to be thus despoiled, but to see others enriched with our spoils, and nevertheless not to cease to do what would please our absent Lover; not to cease following after him; and if by unfaithfulness or surprise we stop for a moment, to redouble our speed, without fearing or contemplating the precipices, although we fall a thousand times, till we are so weary that we lose our strength, and die from continual fatigue; when, perhaps, if our Beloved turns and looks upon us, his glance restores life by the exquisite pleasure it gives; until at last he becomes so cruel that he lets us die for want of help—all this I say, belongs not to this state, but to that which follows. I must remark here, that the degree of which I have been speaking is of very long duration, at least unless God intends the soul to make great advances; and many, as I have said, never pass it.

Chapter 6

Second Degree of the Passive Way of Faith

Second degree of the passive way of faith—Short description of this degree—Entrance into it and useless efforts to avoid it—Gradations and advancements in this degree, in which occur frequent manifestations of Christ to the soul—The uses and abuses which it makes of them, by which it is brought to mystical death, or to the third degree of this passive way of faith.

The torrent having come to the brow of the hill, enters at the same time into the *second degree of the passive way of faith.* This soul, which was so peacefully resting on the mountain top, had no thought of leaving it. However, for want of a declivity, these waters of Heaven by their stay upon earth were becoming tainted; for there is this difference between stagnant waters which have no outlet, and those which are in motion and have an outlet, that the first, with the exception of the sea, and those large lakes which resemble it, grow putrid, and their want of motion causes their destruction. But when, after leaving their source, they have an easy outlet, the more rapidly they flow, the more they are preserved.

You will remember I remarked before of this soul, that as soon as God imparted to it the gift of *passive* faith, he gave it at the same time an instinct to seek after him as its center; but in its unfaithfulness it stifles by its repose this instinct to seek God, and would remain stationary, if God did not revive this instinct by bringing it to the edge of the mountain, whence it is compelled to precipitate itself. At first it is sensible that it has lost that calmness which it expected to retain forever. Its waters, formerly so tranquil, begin to be noisy. A tumult is seen in its waves; they run and dash over. But where do they run? Alas! As they imagine, it is to their own destruction. If it were in their power to desire anything, they would wish to restrain themselves, and return to their former calm. But this is impossible. The declivity is found; they must be precipitated from slope to slope. It is no longer a question of abyss or of loss. The water, that is, the soul, always reappears, and is never lost in this degree. It is embroiled and precipitated; one wave follows another, and the other takes it up and crashes it by its precipitation.

Yet this water finds on the slope of the mountain certain flat places, where it takes a little relaxation. It delights in the clearness of its waters; and it sees that its falls, its course, this breaking of its waves upon the rocks, have served to render it more pure. It finds itself delivered from its noise and storms, and thinks it has now found its resting place; and it believes this the more readily because it cannot doubt that the state through which it has just passed has greatly purified it, for it sees that its waters are clearer, and it no longer perceives the disagreeable odor which certain stagnant parts had given to it on the top of the mountain; it has even acquired a certain insight into its own condition; it has seen by the troubled state of its passions (the waves) that they were not lost, but only asleep. As when it was descending the mountain, on its way to this level, it thought it was losing its way, and had no hope of recovering its lost peace, so now that it no longer hears the dash of its waves, that it finds itself flowing calmly and pleasantly along the sand, it forgets its former trouble, and never imagines there will be a return of it: it sees that it has acquired fresh purity, and does not fear that it will again become soiled; for here it is not stagnant, but flows as gently and brightly as possible.

Ah, poor torrent! You think you have found your resting place, and are firmly established in it! You begin to delight in your waters. The swans glide upon them, and rejoice in their beauty. But what is your surprise while, as you are flowing along so happily, you suddenly encounter a steeper slope, longer and more dangerous than the first! Then the torrent recommences its tumult. Formerly it was only a moderate noise; now it is insupportable. It descends with a crash and a roar greater than ever. It can hardly be said to have a bed, for it falls from rock to rock, and dashes down without order or reason; it alarms everyone by its noise; all fear to approach it. Ah, poor torrent! What will you do? You drag away in your fury all that comes in your way; you feel nothing but the declivity down which you are hurried, and you think you are lost. Nay, do not fear; you are not lost, but the time of your happiness is not yet come. There must be many more disturbances and losses before then; you have but just commenced your course.

At last this dashing torrent feels that it has gained the foot of the mountain and another level spot. It resumes its former calm, and even a deeper one, and after having passed, it may be, years in these changes, it enters the third Degree, before speaking of which, I will touch upon the condition of those who enter it, and the first steps in it. The soul having passed some time in the tranquility of which we have spoken, which it imagines it has secured forever, and having, as it supposes, acquired all the virtues in their full extent, believing all its passions to be dead; when it is expecting to enjoy with the greatest safety a happiness it has no fear of losing, is astonished to find that, instead of mounting higher, or at least remaining in its present position, it comes to the slope of the mountain. It begins, to its amazement, to be sensible of an inclination for the things it had given up. It sees its deep calm suddenly disturbed; distractions come in crowds, one upon another; the soul finds only stones in its path, dryness and aridity. A feeling of distaste comes into prayer. Its passions, which it thought were dead, but which were only asleep, all revive.

It is completely astonished at this change. It would like either to return to the top of the mountain, or at least to remain where it is; but this cannot be. The declivity is found, and the soul must fall (not into sin, but into a privation of the previous degree and of feeling). It does its best to rise after it falls; it does all in its power to restrain itself, and to cling to some devotional exercise; it makes an effort to recover its former peace; it seeks solitude in the hope of recovering it. But its labor is in vain. It resigns itself to suffer its dejection, and hates the sin which has occasioned it. It longs to put things right, but can find no means of doing it; the torrent must go on its way; it drags with it all that is opposed to it. Then, seeing that it no longer finds support in God, it seeks it in the creature; but it finds none; and its unfaithfulness only increases its apprehension. At last, the poor bride, not knowing what to do, weeping everywhere the loss of her Beloved, is filled with astonishment when He again reveals himself to her. At first she is charmed at the sight, as she feared she had lost him forever. She is all the more happy, because she finds that he has brought with him new wealth, a new purity, a great distrust of self. She has no longer the desire to stop, as she formerly had; she goes on continuously, but peacefully and gently, and yet she has fears lest her peace should be disturbed. She trembles lest she should again lose the treasure which is all the dearer to her because she had been so sensible of its loss. She is afraid she may displease him, and that he will leave her again. She tries to be more faithful to him, and not to make an end of the means.

However, this repose carries away the soul, ravishes it, and renders it idle. It cannot help being sensible of its peace, and it desires to be always alone. It has again acquired a spiritual greediness. To rob it of solitude is to rob it of life. It is still more selfish than before, what it possesses being more delightful. It seems to be in a new rest. It is going along calmly, when all at once it comes to another descent, steeper and longer than the former one. It is suddenly seized with a fresh surprise; it endeavors to hold itself back, but in vain; it must fall; it must dash on from rock to rock. It is astonished to find that it has lost its love for prayer and devotion. It does violence to itself by continuing in it. It finds only death at every step. That which formerly revived it is now the cause of its death. Its peace has gone, and has left a trouble and agitation stronger than ever, caused as much by the passions, which revive (though against its will) with the more strength as they appeared the more extinct, as by crosses, which increase outwardly, and which it has no strength to bear. It arms itself with patience; it weeps, groans, and is troubled.

The Bride complains that her Beloved has forsaken her; but her complaints are unheeded. Life has become death to her. All that is good she finds difficult, but has an inclination towards evil which draws her away. But she can find no rest in the creature, having tasted of the Creator. She dashes on more vehemently; and the steeper the rocks, and the greater the obstacles which oppose her course, the more she redoubles her speed. She is like the dove from the ark, which, finding no rest for the sole of its foot, was obliged to return. But alas! What could the poor dove have done if, when it desired to re-enter the ark, Noah had not put out his hand to take it in? It could only have fluttered round about the ark, seeking rest but finding none. So this poor dove flutters round the ark till the Divine Noah, having compassion on her distress, opens the door and receives her to himself. Oh, wonderful and loving invention of the goodness of God! He only eludes the search of the soul to make it flee more quickly to him. He hides himself that he may be sought after. He apparently lets her fall, that he may have the joy of sustaining her and raising her up. Oh, strong and vigorous ones, who have never experienced these artifices of love, these apparent jealousies, these flights, lovely to the soul which has passed them, but terrible to those who experience them! You, I say, who do not know these flights of love, because you are satisfied with the abiding presence of your Beloved; or, if he hide himself, it is for so short a time that you cannot judge of the joy of his presence by the pain of a long absence; you have never experienced your weakness, and your need of his help; but those who are thus forsaken learn to lean no longer on themselves, but only on the Beloved. His rigors have rendered his gentleness the more needful for them.

These persons often commit faults through sheer weakness, and because they are deprived of all sensible support; and these faults so fill them with shame, that, if they could, they would hide themselves from their Beloved. Alas! In the terrible confusion into which they are thrown, he gives them a glimpse of himself. He touches them with his scepter, like another Ahasuerus (Esther 5:2), that they may not die; but his tender caresses only serve to increase their confusion at the thought of having displeased him. At other times he makes them sensible, by his severity, how much their unfaithfulness displeases him. Oh! Then if they could sink into dust, they would. They would do anything to repair the injury done to God; and if, by any slight neglects, which appear crimes to them, they have offended their neighbor, what return are they not willing to make? But it is pitiful to see the state of that one who has driven away her Beloved. She does not cease to run after him, but the faster she goes, the further he seems to leave her behind; and if he stops, it is only for a moment, that she may recover breath. She feels now that she must die; for she no longer finds life in anything; all has become death to her; prayer, reading, conversation—all is dead: she loses the joy of service, or rather, she dies to it, performing it with so much pain and weariness, that it is as death to her. At last, after having fought well, but uselessly, after a long succession of conflicts and rest, of lives and deaths, she begins to see how she has abused the grace of God, and that this state of death is better for her than life; for as she sees her Beloved returning, and finds that she possesses him more purely, and that the state which preceded her rejoicing was a purification for her, she abandons herself willingly to *death,* and to the coming and going of her Beloved, giving him full liberty to go and come as he will. She receives instruction as she is able to bear it. Little by little she loses her joy in herself, and is thus prepared for a new condition.

But before speaking of it, let me say, that in proportion as the soul advances, its joys become short, simple, and pure, and its privations long and agonizing, until it has lost its *own* joy, to find it no more. And this is the *third Degree,* that of *death, burial,* and *decay.* This second Degree ends in death, and goes no further.

CHAPTER 7

Commencement of the Third Degree of the Passive Way of Faith

Section 1: First Degree of the Spoliation of the Soul

Third degree of the passive way of faith, in its commencement, and its progress by various special deaths to a total death, to burial, and to decay—Duration of this transition, in which there must be no advancement beyond faith, nor any receding—Spoliation of the soul, and the three degrees of it—first degree, which concerns gifts, graces, and favors, or ornaments—Its necessity and effects.

You have seen dying persons who, after they have been believed to be dead, have all at once assumed a new strength, and retained it until their death; as a lamp whose oil is spent flickers in the surrounding darkness, but only to die out the more quickly: thus the soul casts out flames, which only last for a moment. It has bravely resisted death; but its oil is spent: the Sun of Righteousness has so withered it up, that it is forced to die. But does this Sun design anything else with its fierce rays, except the

111

consumption of the soul? And the poor soul thus burned thinks that it is frozen! The truth is, that the torment it suffers prevents its recognizing the nature of its pain. So long as the Sun was obscured by clouds, and gave out rays to a certain extent moderated, it felt the heat, and thought it was burning, while in reality it was but slightly warmed: but when the Sun flashed full upon it, then the soul felt itself burning, without believing that it was so much as warmed. O loving deceit! O sweet and cruel Love! Have you lovers only to deceive them thus? You wound these hearts, and then hide your darts, and make them pursue after that which has wounded them. You attract them, and show yourself to them, and when they long to possess you, you flee from them. When you see the soul reduced to the last extremity, and out of breath from its constant pursuit, you show yourself for a moment that it may recover life, only to be killed a thousand times with ever increasing severity.

O rigorous Lover! Innocent murderer! Why dost thou not kill with a single blow? Why give wine to an expiring heart, and restore life in order to destroy it afresh? This is thy sport. Thou woundest to the death; and when thou seest the victim on the point of expiring, thou healest one wound in order to inflict another! Alas! Usually we die but once; and the very cruelest murderers in times of persecution, though they prolonged life, it is true, yet were content to destroy it but once. But thou, less compassionate than they, takest away our life time after time, and restorest it again.

O life, which cannot be lost without so many deaths! O death, which can only be attained by the loss of so many lives! Perhaps this soul, after thou hast devoured it in thy bosom, will enjoy its Beloved. That would be too great happiness for it: it must undergo another torture. It must be *buried* and reduced to *ashes*. But perhaps it will then arrive at the end of its sufferings, for bodies which decay suffer no longer. Oh! It is not thus with the soul: it suffers continually; and burial, decay, and nothingness are even more sensibly felt by it than death itself.

This degree of *death* is extremely long, and as I have said that very few pass the other Degrees, so I say that far less pass this one. Many people have been astonished to see very holy persons, who have lived like angels, die in terrible anguish, and even despairing of their salvation. It is because they have died in this mystical death; and as God wished to promote their advancement, because they were near their end, he redoubled their sorrow. The work of stripping the soul must be left wholly to God. He will do the work perfectly, and the soul will second the spoliation and the death, without putting hindrances in the way. But to do the work for ourselves is to lose everything, and to make a vile state of a divine one. There are persons who, hearing of this spoliation, have effected it for themselves, and remain always stationary; for, as the stripping is their own work, God does not clothe them with himself. The design of God in stripping the soul is to clothe it again. He only impoverishes that he may enrich, and he substitutes *himself* for all that he takes away, which cannot be the case with those whose spoliation is their own work. They indeed lose the gifts of God, but they do not possess God himself in exchange.

In this degree the soul has not learned to let itself be stripped, emptied, impoverished, killed; and all its efforts to sustain itself will but be its irreparable loss, for it is seeking to preserve a life which must be lost. As a person wishing to cause a lamp to die out without extinguishing it, would only have to cease to supply it with oil, and it would die out of itself; but if this person, while persistently expressing a wish that the lamp should go out, continued replenishing it with oil from time to time, the lamp would never go out: it is the same with the soul in this degree, which holds on, however feebly, to life. If it consoles itself, does not suffer itself to be killed, in a word, if it performs any actions of life whatever, it will thereby retard its death. O poor soul! Fight no longer against death, and you will live by your death. I seem to see a drowning man before me; he makes every effort to rise to the surface of the water; he holds on to anything that offers itself to his grasp; he preserves his life so long as his strength holds out; he is only drowned when that strength fails. It is thus with Christians. They endeavor as long as possible to prevent their death; it is only the failure of all power which makes them die. God, who wishes to hasten this death, and who has compassion upon them, cuts off the hands with which they cling to a support, and thus obliges them to sink into the deep. Crosses become multiplied, and the more they increase, the greater is the helplessness to bear them, so that they seem as though they never could be borne. The most painful part of this condition is, that the trouble always begins by some fault in the sufferer, who believes he has brought it upon himself.

113

At last the soul is reduced to utter self-despair. It consents that God should deprive it of the joy of his gifts, and admits that he is just in doing it. It does not even hope to possess these gifts again.

When those who are in this condition see others who are manifestly living in communion with God, their anguish is redoubled, and they sink in the sense of their own nothingness. They long to be able to imitate them, but finding all their efforts useless, they are compelled to die. They say in the language of Scripture, "The thing which I greatly feared is come upon me" (Job 3:25). What! they say, to lose God, and to lose him forever, without the hope of ever finding him again! To be deprived of love for time and for eternity! To be unable to love him whom I know to be so worthy of my affection!

Oh! Is it not sufficient, Divine Lover, to cast off your spouse, to turn away from her, without compelling her to lose love, and lose it, as it seems, forever? She believes she has lost it, and yet she never loved more strongly or more purely. She has indeed lost the vigor, the sensible strength of love; but she has not lost love itself; on the contrary, she possesses it in a greater degree than ever. She cannot believe this, and yet it is easily known; for the heart cannot exist without love. If it does not love God, its affection is concentrated upon some other object: but here the bride of Christ is far from taking pleasure in anything. She regards the revolt of her passions and her involuntary faults as terrible crimes, which draw upon her the hatred of her Beloved. She seeks to cleanse and to purify herself, but she is no sooner washed than, she seems to fall into a slough yet more filthy and polluted than that from which she has just escaped. She does not see that it is because she runs that she contracts defilement, and falls so frequently, yet she is so ashamed to run in this condition, that she does not know where to hide herself. Her garments are soiled; she loses all she has in the race.

Her Bridegroom aids in her spoliation for two reasons. The first: because she has soiled her beautiful garments by her vain complaisances, and has appropriated the gifts of God in reflections of self esteem. The second: because in running, her course will be impeded by this burden of appropriation; even the fear of losing such riches would lessen her speed.

O poor soul! What art thou become? Formerly thou wast the delight of thy Bridegroom, when he took such pleasure in adorning and beautifying thee; now thou art so naked, so ragged, so poor, that thou darest neither to look upon thyself nor to appear before him. Those who gaze upon thee, who, after having so much admired thee, see thee now so disfigured, believe that either thou hast grown mad, or that thou hast committed some great crime, which has caused thy Beloved to abandon thee. They do not see that this jealous Husband, who desires that his bride should be his alone, seeing that she is amusing herself with her ornaments, that she delights in them, that she is in love with herself; seeing this, I say, and that she sometimes ceases looking at him in order to look at herself, and that her love to him is growing cold because her self-love is so strong, is stripping her, and taking away all her beauties and riches from before her eyes.

In the abundance of her wealth, she takes delight in contemplating herself: she sees good qualities in herself, which engage her affection, and alienate it from her Bridegroom. In her foolishness she does not see that she is only fair with the beauties of her Beloved; and that if he removed these, she would be so hideous that she would be frightened at herself. More than this, she neglects to follow him wherever he goes; she fears lest she may spoil her complexion, or lose her jewels. O jealous Love! How well is it that thou comest to chastise this proud one, and to take from her what thou hast given, that she may learn to know herself, and that, being naked and destitute, nothing may impede her course.

Thus, then, our Lord strips the soul little by little, robbing her of her ornaments, all her gifts, positions, and favors—that is, as to her perception or conscious possession of them—which are like jewels that weigh her down; then he takes away her natural capacity for good, which are her garments; after which he destroys her personal beauty, which sets forth divine virtue, which she finds it impossible to practice.

This spoliation commences with the graces, gifts, and favors of conscious love. The bride sees that her husband takes from her, little by little, the riches he had bestowed upon her. At first she is greatly troubled by this loss; but what troubles her the most, is not so much the loss of her riches, as the anger of her Beloved; for she thinks it is in anger that he thus takes back his gifts. She sees the abuse she had made of them, and the delight she had been taking in them, which so fills her with shame that she is ready to die of confusion. She lets him do as he will, and dares not say,

"Why dost thou take from me what thou hast given?" for she sees that she deserves it, and looks on in silence.

Though she keeps silence, it is not so profound now as afterwards; it is broken by mingled sobs and sighs. But she is astonished to find, when she looks at her Bridegroom, that he appears to be angry with her for weeping over his justice towards her, in no longer allowing her the opportunity of abusing his gifts, and for thinking so lightly of the abuse she has made of them. She tries then to let him know that she does not care about the loss of his gifts, if only he will cease his anger towards her. She shows him her tears and her grief at having displeased him. It is true that she is so sensible of the anger of her Beloved that she no longer thinks of her riches. After allowing her to weep for a long time, her Lover appears to be appeased. He consoles her, and with his own hand he dries her tears. What a joy it is to see the new goodness of her Beloved, after what she has done! Yet he does not restore her former riches, and she does not long for them, being only too happy to be looked upon, consoled, and caressed by him. At first she receives his caresses with so much confusion, that she dare not lift her eyes, but forgetting her past woes in her present happiness, she loses herself in the new caresses of her Beloved, and thinking no more of her past miseries, she glories and rests in these caresses, and thereby compels the Bridegroom to be angry again, and to despoil her anew.

It must be observed that God despoils the loss little by little; and the weaker the souls may be, the longer the spoliation continues; while the stronger they are, the sooner it is completed, because God despoils them oftener and of more things at once. But however rough this spoliation may be, it only touches superfluities on the outside, that is to say, gifts, graces, and favors. This leading of God is so wonderful, and is the result of such deep love to the soul, that it would never be believed, except by those who have experienced it; for the heart is so full of itself, and so permeated with self esteem, that if God did not treat it thus, it would be lost.

It will perhaps be asked, if the gifts of God are productive of such evil consequences, why are they given? God gives them, in the fullness of his goodness, in order to draw the soul from sin, from attachment to the creature, and to bring it back to himself. But these same gifts with which he gratifies it—that he may wean it from earth and from self to love him, at least from gratitude—we use to excite our self love and self admiration, to amuse ourselves with them; and self love is so deeply rooted in man, that it is augmented by these gifts; for he finds in himself new charms, which he had not discovered before; he delights in them, and appropriates to himself what belongs only to God. It is true, God could deliver him from it, but he does not do it, for reasons known only to himself. The soul, thus despoiled by God, loses a little of its self love, and begins to see that it was not so rich as it fancied, but that all its virtue was in Christ; it sees that it has abused his grace, and consents that he should take back his gifts. The bride says, "I shall be rich with the riches of my Bridegroom, and though he may keep them, yet, from my union in heart and will with him, they will still be mine." She is even glad to lose these gifts of God; she finds herself unencumbered, better fitted for walking. Gradually she becomes accustomed to this spoliation; she knows it has been good for her; she is no longer grieved because of it; and, as she is so beautiful, she satisfies herself that she will not cease to please her Bridegroom by her natural beauty and her simple garments, as much as she could with all her ornaments.

Section 2: Second Degree of the Spoliation of the Soul

Second degree of the spoliation of the soul, as to its garments, or its facility for the exterior practice of virtue—its causes, which are the appropriation of these virtues, and satisfaction in them, instead of the recognition of natural helplessness, and absence of all good in self.

When the poor bride is expecting always to live in peace, in spite of this loss, and sees clearly the good which has resulted to her from it, and the harm she had done to herself by the bad use which she had made of the gifts which now have been taken from her, she is completely astonished to find that the Bridegroom, who had only given her temporary peace because of her weakness, comes with yet greater violence to tear off her clothing from her.

Alas, poor bride! What wilt thou do now? This is far worse than before, for these garments are necessary to her, and it is contrary to all propriety to suffer herself to be stripped of them. Oh! It is now that she makes all the resistance in her power. She brings forward all the reasons why her Bridegroom should not thus leave her naked: she tells him that it will bring reproach upon himself. "Alas!" she cries,

> I have lost all the virtues which thou hast bestowed upon me, thy gifts, the sweetness of thy love! But still I was able to make an outward profession of virtue; I engaged in works of charity; I prayed assiduously, even though I was deprived of thy sensible benefits: but I cannot consent to lose all this. I was still clothed according to my position, and looked upon by the world as thy bride: but if I lose my garments, it will bring shame upon Thee.

> [Christ replies:] It matters not, poor soul; thou must consent to this loss also: thou dost not yet know thyself; thou believest that thy raiment is thine own, and that thou canst use it as thou wilt. But though I acquired it at such a cost, thou hast given it back to me as if it were a recompense on thy part for the labors I have endured for thee. Let it go; thou must lose it.

The soul having done its best to keep it, lets it go, little by little, and finds itself gradually despoiled. It finds no inclination for anything; on the contrary, all is distasteful to it. Formerly it had aversions and difficulties, without absolute powerlessness; but here all power is taken from it: its strength of body and mind fails entirely; the inclination for better things alone remains, and this is the last robe, which must finally be lost.

This is done very gradually, and the process is extremely painful, because the bride sees all the while that it has been caused by her own folly. She dares not speak, lest she may irritate the Bridegroom, whose anger is worse to her than death. She begins to know herself better, to see that she is nothing in herself, and that all belongs to her Bridegroom. She begins to distrust herself, and, little by little, she loses her self esteem.

But she does not yet hate herself, for she is still beautiful, though naked. From time to time she casts a pitiful look towards the Bridegroom, but she says not a word: she is grieved at his anger. It seems to her that the spoliation would be of little moment if she had not offended him, and if she had not rendered herself unworthy to wear her nuptial robes.

If she was confused when at the first her riches were taken from her, her confusion at the sight of her nakedness is infinitely more painful. She cannot bear to appear before her Bridegroom, so deep is her shame. But she must remain, and run hither and thither in this state. What! Is it not even permitted to her to hide herself? No; she must appear thus in public. The world begins to think less highly of her. It says, "Is this that bride who was once the admiration of angels and of men? See how she has fallen!" These words increase her confusion, because she is well aware that her Bridegroom has dealt justly with her. She does what she can to induce him to clothe her a little, but he will do nothing, after having thus stripped her of all, for her garments would satisfy her by covering her, and would prevent her seeing herself as she is.

It is a great surprise to a soul that thinks itself far advanced towards perfection to see itself thus despoiled all at once. It imagines the old sins, from which it was once purged, must have returned. But it is mistaken: the secret is, that she was so hidden by her garments as to be unable to see what she was. It is a terrible thing for a soul to be thus stripped of the gifts and graces of God, and it is impossible that any should know or imagine what it is without the actual experience of it.

Section 3: Third Degree of Spoliation

Third degree of the spoliation of the soul, which concerns its beauty, or the perceptible action of divine virtue—How God thus leads the soul to self despair and to true purity—Interval of rest, followed by the increase of the preceding operations, till they end in mystic death.

All this would be but little if the bride still retained her beauty; but the Bridegroom robs her of that also. Hitherto she has been despoiled of gifts, graces, and favors (facility for good): she has lost all good works, such as outward charity, care for the poor, readiness to help others, but she has not lost the divine virtues. Here, however, these too must be lost, so far as their practice is concerned, or rather the habit of exercising them, as acquired by herself, in order to appear fair: in reality, they are all the while being more strongly implanted. She loses virtue as virtue, but it is only that she may find it again in *Christ*. This degraded bride becomes, as she imagines, filled with pride. She, who was so patient, who suffered so easily, finds that she can suffer nothing. Her senses revolt her by continual distractions. She can no longer restrain herself by her own efforts, as formerly; and what is worse, she contracts defilement at every step. She complains to her Beloved that the watchmen that go about the city have found her and wounded her (Cant. 5:7). I ought, however, to say that persons in this condition do not sin willingly. God usually reveals to them such a deep seated corruption within themselves, that they cry with Job, "Oh, that thou wouldest hide me in the grave, that thou wouldest keep me in secret, until thy wrath be past!" (Job 14:13).

It must not be supposed that either here or at any other stage of progress God suffers the soul really to fall into sin; and so truly is this the case, that though they appear in their own eyes the most miserable sinners, yet they can discover no definite sin of which they are guilty, and only accuse themselves of being full of misery, and of having only sentiments contrary to their desires. It is to the glory of God that, when he makes the soul most deeply conscious of its inward corruption, he does not permit it to fall into sin. What makes its sorrow so terrible is, that it is overwhelmed with a sense of the purity of God, and that purity makes the smallest imperfection appear as a heinous sin, because of the infinite distance between the purity of God and the impurity of the creature.

The soul sees that it was originally created pure by God, and that it has contracted not only the original sin of Adam, but thousands of actual sins, so that its confusion is greater than can be expressed. The reason why Christians in this condition are despised by others, is not to be found in any particular faults which are observed in them, but because, as they no longer manifest the same ardor and fidelity which formerly distinguished them, the greatness of their fall is judged from this, which is a great mistake.

Let this serve to explain or modify any statements or representations in the sequel, which may appear to be expressed too strongly, and which those who do not understand the experience might be liable to misinterpret. Observe, also, that when I speak of *corruption,* of *decay,* etc., I mean the destruction of the old man by the central conviction, and by an intimate experience of the depth of impurity and selfishness which there is in the heart of man, which, bringing him to see himself as he is apart from God, causes him to cry with David, "I am a worm and no man" (Ps. 22:6), and with Job,

> If I wash myself with snow water, and make my hands never so clean, yet shalt thou plunge me in the ditch, and mine own clothes shall abhor me. (Job 9:30–31)

It is not, then, that this poor bride commits the faults of which she imagines herself guilty, for in heart she was never purer than now; but her senses and natural powers, particularly the senses, being unsupported, wander away. Besides which, as the speed of her course towards God redoubles, and she forgets herself more, it is not to be wondered at that in running she soils herself in the muddy places through which she passes; and as all her attention is directed towards her Beloved, although she does not perceive it by reason of her own condition, she thinks no more of herself, and does not notice where she steps. So that, while believing herself most guilty, she does not willingly commit a single sin; though all her sins appear voluntary to herself, they are rather faults of surprise, which often she does not see until after they are committed. She cries to her Bridegroom, but he does not heed her, at least not perceptibly, though he sustains her with an invisible hand. Sometimes she tries to do better, but then she becomes worse; for the design of her Bridegroom in letting her fall *without wounding herself* (Ps. 37:24) is that she should lean no longer on herself; that she should recognize her helplessness; that she should sink into complete self despair; and that she should say, "My soul chooseth death rather than life" (Job 7:15). It is here that the soul begins truly to *hate itself*, and to *know itself* as it would never have done if it had not passed through this experience.

All our natural knowledge of self, whatever may be its degree, is not sufficient to cause us really to hate ourselves.

> He that loveth his life shall lose it; and he that hateth his life in this world, shall keep it unto life eternal. (John 12:25)

It is only such an experience as this which can reveal to the soul its infinite depth of misery. No other way can give true purity; if it give any at all, it is only superficial, and not in the depth of the heart, where the impurity is seated.

Here God searches the inmost recesses of the soul for that hidden impurity which is the effect of the self esteem and self love which he designs to destroy. Take a sponge which is full of impurities, wash it as much as you will, you will clean the outside, but you will not render it clean throughout unless you press it, in order to squeeze out all the filth. This is what God does. He squeezes the soul in a painful manner, but he brings out from it that which was the most deeply hidden.

I say, then, that this is the only way in which we can be purified radically; and without it we should always be filthy, though outwardly we might appear very clean. It is necessary that God should make the soul thoroughly sensible of its condition. We could never believe, without the experience, of what nature left to itself capable. Yes, indeed, our own being, abandoned to itself, is worse than all devils. Therefore we must not believe that the soul in this state of misery is abandoned by God. It was never better sustained; but nature is, as it were, left a little alone, and makes all these ravages without the soul in itself taking any part in them. This poor desolate bride, running hither and thither in search of her Beloved, not only soils herself grievously, as I have said, by falling into faults of surprise and self esteem, but she wounds herself with the thorns that come in her way. She becomes so wearied at length that she is forced to die in her race for want of help; that is, to expect nothing from herself or her own activity.

That which is productive of the highest good to the soul in this condition is that God manifests no pity towards it; and when he desires to promote its advancement, he lets it run even to death; if he stops it for a moment, by doing which he ravishes and revives it, it is because of its weakness, and in order that its weariness may not compel it to rest.

When he sees that it is becoming disheartened and inclined to give up the race altogether, he looks upon it for a moment, and the poor bride finds herself wounded anew by this look. She would willingly say to him, "Alas! Why hast thou thus compelled me to run? Oh, that I could find thee; and see thee face to face!" But alas! when she seems to lay hold of him, he flees from her again. "I sought thee," she cries, "but I found thee not" (Cant. 3:1).

As this look from her Bridegroom has increased her love, she redoubles her speed in order to find him: nevertheless she was delayed just so long as the look lasted, that is, in sensible joy. This is why the Bridegroom does not often cast such looks upon her, and only when he sees that her courage is failing.

The soul then dies at the end of its race, because all its active strength is exhausted; for though it had been passive, it had not lost its active strength, though it had been unconscious of it. The bride said, "Draw me, we will run after thee" (Cant.1:3). She ran indeed, but how? By the loss of all; as the sun travels incessantly, yet without quitting his repose. In this condition she so hates herself, that she can hardly suffer herself. She thinks her Bridegroom has good reason to treat her as he does, and that it is his indignation against her which makes him leave her. She does not see that it is in order to make her run that he flees, that it is in order that he may purify her that he suffers her to become so soiled. When we put iron in the fire, to purify it and to purge it from its dross, it appears at first to be tarnished and blackened, but afterwards it is easy to see that it has been purified. Christ only makes his bride experience her own weakness, that she may lose all strength and all support in herself, and that, in her self despair, he may carry her in his arms, and she may be willing to be thus borne; for whatever her course may be, she walks as a child; but when she is in God, and is borne by him, her progress is infinite, since it is that of God himself.

In addition to all this degradation, the bride sees others adorned with her spoils. When she sees a holy soul, she dare not approach it; she sees it adorned with all the ornaments which her Bridegroom has taken from her; but though she admires it, and sinks into the depths of nothingness, she cannot desire to have these ornaments again, so conscious is she of her unworthiness to wear them. She thinks it would be a profanation to put them upon a person so covered with mud and defilement. She even rejoices to see that, if she fills her Beloved with horror, there are others in whom he can take delight, and whom she regards as infinitely happy in having gained the love of her God: as for the ornaments, though she sees others decorated with them, she does not suppose that these are the sources of their happiness. If she sees any blessedness in the possession of them, it is because they are the tokens of the love of her Beloved. When she is thus sensible of her littleness in the presence of such as these, whom she regards as queens, she does not know the good which will result to her from this nakedness, death, and decay. Her Bridegroom only unclothes her that he may be himself her clothing: "Put ye on the Lord Jesus Christ," says S. Paul (Rom. 13:14). He only kills her that he may be her life: "If we be dead with Christ, we believe that we shall also live with him." He only annihilates her that she may be transformed in himself.

This loss of virtue is only brought about by degrees, as well as the other losses, and this apparent inclination for evil is involuntary; for that evil which makes us so vile in our own eyes is really no evil at all.

The things which bring defilement to these persons are certain faults which only lie in the feelings. As soon as they see the beauty of a virtue, they seem to be incessantly falling into the contrary vice: for example, if they love truth, they speak hastily or with exaggeration, and fancy they lie at every moment, although in fact they do but speak against their sentiments; and it is thus with all the other virtues, the more important these virtues are, and the more strongly they cling to them, because they appear the more essential, the greater is the force with which they are torn from them.

Section 4: Entrance into Mystical Death

Entrance of the soul into mystic death, as to its sensibilities, powers, and even its perceived foundation—Important observations on this condition.

This poor soul, after having lost its all, must at last lose *its own life* by an utter self-despair, or rather it must die worn out by terrible fatigue. Prayer in this degree is extremely painful, because the soul being no longer able to make use of its own powers, of which it seems to be entirely deprived, and God having taken from it a certain sweet and profound calm which supported it, is left like those poor children whom we see running here and there in search of bread, yet finding no one to supply their need. So that the power of prayer seems to be as entirely lost as if we had never possessed it; but with this difference, that we feel the pain occasioned by the loss, because we have proved its value by its possession, while others are not sensible of the loss, because they have never known its enjoyment.

The soul, then, can find no support in the creature; and if it feels itself carried away by the things of earth, it is only by impetuosity, and it can find nothing to satisfy it. Not that it does not seek to abandon itself to the things in which it formerly delighted; but alas! it finds in them nothing but bitterness, so that it is glad to leave them again, taking nothing back but sadness at its own unfaithfulness.

The *imagination* goes altogether astray, and is scarcely ever at rest. The three powers of the soul, the *understanding*, the *memory*, and the *will*, by degrees lose their life, so that at length they become altogether dead, which is very painful to the soul, especially as regards the will, which had been tasting I know not what of sweetness and tranquility, which comforted the other powers in their deadness and powerlessness.

This unexplainable something which sustains the soul at its foundation, as it were, is the hardest of all to lose, and that which the soul endeavors the most strenuously to retain; for as it is too delicate, so it appears the more divine and necessary: it would consent willingly to be deprived of the two other powers, and even of the will, so far as it is a distinct and perceived thing, if only this something might be left; for it could bear all its labors if it may have within itself the witness that it is born of God.

However, this must be lost, like the rest—that is, as to the sentiment—and then the soul enters into the *sensible* realization of all the misery with which it is filled. And it is this which really produces *the spiritual death*; for whatever misery the soul might endure, if this, I know not what, were not lost, it would not die; and if, on the other hand, this were lost without the soul being conscious of its misery, it would be supported, and would not die. It can easily understand that it must give up all dependence upon its own feelings or upon any natural support, but to lose an almost imperceptible comfort, and to fall from weakness, to fall into the mire, to this it cannot consent. This is where reason fails, this is where terrible fears fill the heart, which seems to have only sufficient life to be sensible of its death.

It is, then, the loss of this imperceptible support, and the experience of this misery, which causes death.

We should be very careful, in such times as these, not to let our senses be led away willingly to creatures, seeking willingly consolation and diversion. I say *willingly*, for we are incapable of mortifications and attentions reflected upon ourselves, and the more we have mortified ourselves, the stronger will be the bearing in the contrary direction, without being aware of it. Like a madman, who goes wandering about: if you attempt to keep him too rigorously within bounds, apart from its being useless, it would retard his death.

What must we do then? We must be careful to give no support to the senses, to suffer them, and to let them find recreation in innocent ways; for as they are not capable of an inward operation, by endeavoring to restrain them we should injure health, and even mental strength. What I say applies only to this degree; for if we were to make this use of the senses in the time of the strength and activity of grace, we should do wrong; and our Lord himself in his goodness makes us see the conduct that we should pursue; for at first, he puts such a pressure on the senses, they have no liberty. They only have to desire something in order to be deprived of it; God orders it thus that the senses may be drawn from their imperfect operation, to be confined within the heart; and in severing them outwardly, he binds them inwardly so gently, that it costs them little to be deprived of everything; they even find more pleasure in this deprivation than in the possession of all things. But when they are sufficiently purified, God, who wishes to draw the soul out of itself with a contrary movement, permits the senses to expand outwardly, which appears to the soul as a great impurity. However, it has now happened seasonably [at the right time], and to endeavor to order things otherwise, would be to purify ourselves in a different way from that which God desires, and therefore to defile ourselves anew.

This does not prevent our making mistakes in this outward development of the senses; but the confusion which it occasions us, and our fidelity in making use of it, is the furnace in which we are most quickly purified, by dying the soonest to ourselves. It is here also that we lose the esteem of men. They look on us with contempt, and say, "Are not these the persons whom we formerly admired? How are they become thus disfigured?" "Alas!" we reply, "look not upon me, because I am black" (Cant. 1:6). "It is the sun which has thus discolored me." It is at this point that we suddenly enter the third Degree, that of burial and decay.

CHAPTER 8

Third Degree of the Passive Way of Faith, in Its Consummation

Third degree of the passive way of faith in its consummation—Consummated state of spiritual death—Burial—Decay—Advice as to the conduct of persons in these conditions, which are followed by a new life.

The torrent, as we have said, has passed through every imaginable vicissitude [sudden or unexpected change]. It has been dashed against rocks; indeed, its course has been but a succession of falls from rock to rock; but it has always reappeared, and we have never seen it really lost. Now it begins to lose itself in gulf after gulf. Formerly it still had a course, though it was so precipitate, so confused, and so irregular; but here it is engulfed with a yet greater precipitation in unsearchable depths. For a long time it disappears altogether from view, then we perceive it slightly, but more by hearing than by sight, and it only appears to be again precipitated in a deeper gulf. It falls from abyss to abyss, from precipice to precipice, until at last it falls into the depths of the sea, where, losing all form, it is lost, to be found no more, having become one with the sea itself. The soul, after many deaths, expires at last in the arms of Love; but it does not even perceive those arms. It has no sooner expired, than it loses all vital action, all desire, inclination, tendency, choice, repugnance, and aversion. As it draws near to death, it grows weaker; but its life, though languishing and agonizing, is still life, and "while there is life there is hope," even though death be inevitable. The torrent must be buried out of sight.

O God! What is this? What were only precipices become abysses. The soul falls into a depth of misery from which there is no escape. At first this abyss is small, but the further the soul advances, the stronger does it appear, so that it goes from bad to worse; for it is to be remarked, that when we first enter a degree, there clings to us much that we have brought in with us, and at the end we already begin to feel symptoms of that which is to come. It is also noticeable that each degree contains within it an infinitude of others.

A man, after his death and before his burial, is still among the living: he still has the face of a man, though he is an object of terror; thus the soul, in the commencement of this degree, still bears some resemblance to what it was before; there remains in it a certain secret impression of God, as there remains in a dead body a certain animal heat which gradually leaves it. The soul still practices devotion and prayer, but this is soon taken away from it. It must lose not only all prayer, every gift of God, but God himself to all appearance—that is, so far as he was possessed selfishly by the *ego*—and not lose him for one, two, or three years, but forever. All facility for good, all active virtue, are taken from it; it is left naked and despoiled of everything. The world, which formerly esteemed it so much, begins to fear it. Yet it is no visible sin which produces the contempt of men, but a powerlessness to practice its former good works with the same facility. Formerly whole days were spent in the visitation of the sick, often even against natural inclination; such works as these can be practiced no longer.

The soul will soon be in an entire oblivion. Little by little, it loses everything in such a degree, that it is altogether impoverished. The world tramples it underfoot, and thinks no more of it. O poor soul! Thou must see thyself treated thus, and see it with terror, without being able to prevent it. It must suffer itself to be buried, covered with earth, and trodden underfoot by all men.

It is here that heavy crosses are borne, and all the heavier that they are believed to be merited. The soul begins to have a horror of itself. God casts it so far off, that he seems determined to abandon it forever. Poor soul! Thou must be patient, and remain in thy sepulcher. It is content to remain there, though in terrible suffering, because it sees no way of escape from it; and it sees, too, that it is its only fit place, all others being even sadder to it. It flees from men, knowing that they regard it with aversion. They look upon this forlorn Bride as an outcast, who has lost the grace of God, and who is only fit to be buried in the earth.

The heart endures its bitterness; but, alas! How sweet this state is even now, and how easy it would be to remain in the sepulcher, if it were not necessary to decay! The old man becomes gradually corrupted; formerly there were weaknesses and failings, now the soul sees a depth of corruption of which it had hitherto been ignorant, for it could not imagine what were its self esteem and selfishness. O, God! What horror this soul suffers in seeing itself thus decaying! All troubles, the contempt and aversion of man, affect it no longer. It is even insensible to the deprivation of the Sun of Righteousness; it knows that his light does not penetrate the tomb. But to feel its own corruption, that it cannot endure. What would it not rather suffer? But it must experience, to the very depths of its being, what it is.

And yet, if I could decay without being seen by God, I should be content: what troubles me is the horror which I must cause him by the sight of my corruption. But, poor desolate one! What canst thou do? It should suffice thee, one would think, to *bear* this corruption, without *loving* it: but now thou art not even sure that thou dost not desire it! The soul is in darkness, without being able to judge whether its terrible thoughts proceed from itself or from the evil one.

It is no longer troubled at being cast off by God; it is so conscious of its demerit, that it consents to the deprivation of the sensible presence of God. But it cannot endure the thought that the taint of its corruption reaches even to God. It does not wish to sin. "Let me decay," is its cry, "and find my home in the depths of hell, if only I may be kept free from sin." It no longer thinks of love, for it believes itself to be incapable of affection. It is, in its own opinion, worse than when it was in a state of nature, since it is in the state of corruption usual to the body deprived of life.

At length by degrees the soul becomes accustomed to its corruption: it feels it less, and finds it natural, except at certain times, when it is tried by various temptations, whose terrible impressions cause it much anguish. Ah, poor torrent! Wast thou not better off on the mountain top than here? Thou hadst then some slight corruption, it is true; but now, though thou flowest rapidly, and nothing can stop thee, thou passest through such filthy places, so tainted with sulphur and salt-petre, that thou bearest away their odors with thee.

At last the soul is reduced to a state of nothingness, and has become like a person who does not exist, and never will exist; it does nothing, either good or ill. Formerly it thought of itself, now it thinks no longer. All that is of grace is done as if it were of nature, and there is no longer either pain or pleasure. All that there is, is that its ashes remain as ashes, without the hope of ever being anything but ashes: it is utterly dead, and nothing affects it either from without or within—that is, it is no longer troubled by any sensible impressions. At last, reduced to nonentity, there is found in the ashes *a germ of immortality*, which lives beneath these ashes, and in due time will manifest its life. But the soul is in ignorance of it, and never expects to be revived or raised from the dead.

The faithfulness of the soul in this condition consists in letting itself be buried, crushed, trampled on, without making any more movement than a corpse, without seeking in any way to prevent its putrefaction. There are those who wish to apply balm to themselves. No, no; leave yourselves as you are. You must know your corruption, and see the infinite depth of depravity that is in you. To apply balm is but to endeavor by good works to hide your corruption. Oh, do it not! You will wrong yourselves. God can suffer you; why cannot you suffer yourselves? The soul, reduced to nothingness, must remain in it, without wishing to change its state; and it is then that the torrent loses itself in the sea, never to find itself in itself again, but to become one with the sea. It is then that this corpse feels without feeling, that it is gradually reanimated, and assumes *a new life*; but this is done so gradually that, it seems like a dream. And this brings us to the last Degree, which is the commencement of the *divine and truly inner life*, including numberless smaller degrees, and in which the advancement is infinite: just as this torrent can perpetually advance in the sea, and imbibe more of its nature, the longer it remains in it.

Chapter 9

*Fourth Degree of the Passive Way of Faith,
Which Is the Commencement of the Divine Life*

*Fourth degree of the passive way of faith, which is the commencement of the
divine life—Transition from the human state to the divine, and to the resurrection of the soul in God—Description of this life and of its properties, gradations, identity, indifference—Sentiments of the soul—Its existence in God—its
peace, etc.—Power and views with regard to others, to itself, to its condition, to
its actions, to its words, to its faults—Mind of Christ—Various observations.*

When the torrent begins to lose itself in the sea, it can easily be distinguished. Its movement is perceptible, until at length it gradually loses all form
of its own, to take that of the sea. So the soul, leaving this degree, and beginning to lose itself, yet retains something of its own; but in a short time it loses
all that it had peculiar to itself. The corpse which has been reduced to ashes is
still dust and ashes; but if another person were to swallow those ashes, they
would no longer have an identity, but would form part of the person who had
taken them. The soul hitherto, though dead and buried, has retained its own
being; it is only in this degree that it is really taken out of itself.

131

All that has taken place up to this point has been in the individual capacity of the creature; but here the creature is taken out of his own capacity to receive an infinite capacity in God himself. And as the torrent, when it enters the sea, loses its own being in such a way that it retains nothing of it, and takes that of the sea, or rather is taken out of itself to be lost in the sea; so this soul loses the human in order that it may lose itself in the divine, which becomes its being and its subsistence, not essentially, but mystically. Then this torrent possesses all the treasures of the sea, and is as glorious as it was formerly poor and miserable.

It is in the tomb that the soul begins to resume life, and the light enters insensibly. Then it can be truly said that

> The people which sat in darkness saw great light; and to them which sat
> in the region and shadow of death, light is sprung up." (Matt. 4:16)

There is a beautiful figure of this resurrection in Ezekiel (chap. 37), where the dry bones gradually assume life: and then there is that other passage:

> The hour is coming, and now is, when the dead shall hear the voice of
> the Son of God; and they that hear shall live." (John 5:25)

O you who are coming out of the sepulcher! you feel within yourselves a germ of life springing up little by little: you are quite astonished to find a secret strength taking possession of you: your ashes are reanimated: you feel yourselves to be in a new country. The poor soul, which only expected to remain at rest in its grave, receives an agreeable surprise. It does not know what to think: it supposes that the sun must have shed upon it a few scattered rays through some opening or chink, whose brightness will only last for a moment. It is still more astonished when it feels this secret vigor permeating its entire being, and finds that it gradually receives a new life, to lose it no more forever, unless it be by the most flagrant unfaithfulness.

But this new life is not like the former one: it is a life in God. It is a perfect life. The soul lives no longer and works no longer of itself, but only God lives, acts, and operates in it (Gal. 2:20); and this goes on increasing, so that it becomes perfect with God's perfection, rich with God's riches, and loving with God's love.

The soul sees now that whatever it owned formerly had been in its own possession. Now it no longer possesses, but is possessed: it only takes a new life in order to lose it in God; or rather it only lives with the life of God; and, as he is the principle of life, the soul can want nothing. What a gain it has made by all its losses! It has lost the created for the Creator, the nothing for the All in All. All things are given to it, not in itself, but in God; not to be possessed by itself, but to be possessed by God. Its riches are immense, for they are God himself. It feels its capacity increasing day by day to immensity: every virtue is restored to it, but in God.

It must be remarked, that as it was only despoiled by degrees, so it is only enriched and vivified by degrees. The more it loses itself in God, the greater its capacity becomes; just as the more the torrent loses itself in the sea, the more it is enlarged, having no other limits than those of the sea: it participates in all its properties. The soul becomes strong and firm: it has lost all means, but it has found the end. This divine life becomes quite natural to it. As it no longer feels itself, sees itself, or knows itself, so it no longer sees or understands or distinguishes anything of God as distinct or outside of itself. It is no longer conscious of love, or light, or knowledge; it only knows that God is, and that it no longer lives except in God. All devotion is action, and all action is devotion: all is the same; the soul is indifferent to all, for all is equally God. Formerly it was necessary to exercise virtue in order to perform virtuous works. Here all distinction of action is taken away, the actions having no virtue in themselves, but all being God, the meanest action equally with the greatest, provided it is in the order of God and at his time. For all that might be of the natural choice, and not in this order, would have another effect, leading the soul out of God by unfaithfulness. Not that it would be brought out of its degree or its loss, but out of the divine plan, which makes all things one, and all things God. So the soul is *indifferent* as to whether it be in one state or another, in one place or another: all is the same to it, and it lets itself be carried along naturally. It ceases to think, to wish, or to choose for itself; but remains content, without care or anxiety, no longer distinguishing its inner life to speak of it. Indeed it may be said not to possess one: it is no longer in itself; it is all in God. It is not necessary for it to shut itself up within itself; it does not hope to find anything there, and does not seek for it. If a person were altogether penetrated with the sea, having sea within and without, above and below, on every side, he would not prefer one place to another, all being the same to him. So the soul does not trouble itself to seek anything or to do anything; that is, of itself, by itself, or for itself. It remains as it is. But what does it do? Nothing—always nothing. It does what it is made to do, it suffers what it is made to suffer. Its peace is unchangeable, but always natural. It has, as it were, passed into a state of nature; and yet how different from those altogether without God!

The difference is, that it is compelled to action by God without being conscious of it, whereas formerly it was nature that acted. It seems to itself to do neither right nor wrong, but it lives satisfied, peaceful, doing what it is made to do in a steady and resolute manner.

God alone is its guide; for at the time of its loss, it lost its own will. And if you were to ask what are its desires, it could not tell. It can choose for itself no longer: all desire is taken away, because, having found its center, the heart loses all natural inclination, tendency, and activity, in the same way as it loses all repugnance and contrariety. The torrent has no longer either a declivity or a movement: it is in repose, and at its end.

But with what satisfaction is this soul satisfied? With the satisfaction of God, immense, general, without knowing or understanding what it is that satisfies it; for here all sentiments, tastes, views, particular opinions, however delicate they may be, are taken from it: that certain vague, indefinable something, which formerly occupied without occupying it, is gone, and nothing remains to it. But this insensibility is very different to that of death, burial, and decay. That was a *deprivation of life*, a distaste, a separation, the powerlessness of the dying united with the insensibility of the dead; but this is an *elevation* above all these things, which does not remove them, but renders them useless. A dead man is deprived of all the functions of life by the powerlessness of death; but if he were to be raised gloriously, he would be full of life, without having the power to preserve it by means of the senses: and being placed above all means by virtue of his germ of immortality, he would no longer feel that which animated him, although he would know himself to be alive.

In this degree God cannot be tasted, seen, or felt, being no longer distinct from ourselves, but one with us. The soul has neither inclination nor taste for anything: in the period of death and burial it experienced this, but in a very different manner. Then it arose from distaste and powerlessness, but now it is the effect of *plenitude* and *abundance*; just as, if a person could live on air, he would be full without feeling his plenitude, or knowing in what way he had been satisfied; he would not be empty and unable to eat or to taste, but free from all necessity of eating by reason of his satisfaction, without knowing how the air, entering by all his pores, had penetrated equally at all parts.

The soul here is in God, as in the air which is natural to it, and it is no more sensible of its fullness than we are of the air we breathe. Yet it is full, and nothing is wanting to it; therefore all its desires are taken from it. Its peace is great, but not as it was before. Formerly it was an inanimate peace, a certain sepulture, from which there sometimes escaped exhalations which troubled it. When it was reduced to ashes, it was at peace; but it was a barren peace, like that of a corpse, which would be at peace in the midst of the wildest storms of the sea: it would not feel them, and would not be troubled by them, its state of death rendering it insensible. But here the soul is raised, as it were, to a mountain top, from which it sees the waves rolling and tossing, without fearing their attacks; or rather it is at the bottom of the sea, where there is always tranquility, even while the surface is agitated. The senses may suffer their sorrows, but at the center there is always the same calm tranquility, because he who possesses it is immutable.

This, of course, supposes the faithfulness of the soul; for in whatever state it may be, it is possible for it to recede and fall back into itself. But here the soul progresses infinitely in God; and it is possible for it to advance incessantly; just as, if the sea had no bottom, any one falling into it would sink to infinitude, and going down to greater and greater depths of the ocean, would discover more and more of its beauties and treasures. It is even thus with the soul whose home is in God.

But what must it do in order to be faithful to God? Nothing, and less than nothing. It must simply suffer itself to be possessed, acted upon, and moved without resistance, remaining in the state which is natural to it, waiting for what every moment may bring to it, and receiving it from him, without either adding to or taking from it; letting itself be led at all times and to any place, regardless of sight or reason, and without thinking of either; letting itself go naturally into all things, without considering what would be best or most plausible; remaining in the state of evenness and stability in which God has placed it, without being troubled to do anything; but leaving to God the care of providing its opportunities, and of doing all for it; not making definite acts of abandonment, but simply resting in the state of abandonment in which it already is, and which is natural to it.

The soul is unable to act in any way of itself without a consciousness of unfaithfulness. It possesses all things by having nothing. It finds a facility for every duty, for speaking and for acting, no longer in its own way, but in God's. Its faithfulness does not consist in ceasing from all activity, like one who is dead, but in doing nothing except by the principle which animates it. A soul in this state has no inclination of its own in anything, but lets itself go as it is led, and beyond that does nothing. It cannot speak of its state, for it does not see it; though there is so much that is extraordinary, it is no longer as it was in the former degrees, where the creature had some part in it, that which was in a great measure its own; but here the most wonderful things are perfectly natural, and are done without thought. It is the same principle that gives life to the soul which acts *in it* and *through it*. It has a sovereign power over the hearts of those around it, but not of itself. As nothing belongs to it, it can make no reserves; and if it can say nothing of a state so divine, it is not because it fears vanity, for that no longer exists; it is rather because what it has, while possessing nothing, passes all expression by its extreme simplicity and purity. Not that there are not many things which are but the accessories of this condition, and not the center, of which it can easily speak. These accessories are like the crumbs which fall from that eternal feast of which the soul begins to partake in time; they are but the sparks which prove the existence of a furnace of fire and flame; but it is impossible to speak of the principle and the end, because only so much can be imparted as God is pleased to give at the moment to be either written or spoken.

It may be asked, "Is the soul unconscious of its faults, or does it commit none?" It does commit them, and is more conscious of them than ever, especially in the commencement of its new life. The faults committed are often more subtle and delicate than formerly. The soul knows them better, because its eyes are open; but it is not troubled by them, and can do nothing to rid itself of them. It is true that, when it has been guilty of unfaithfulness or sin, it is sensible of a certain cloud; but it passes over, without the soul itself doing anything to dispel it, or to cleanse itself; apart from which, any efforts it might make would be useless, and would only serve to increase its impurity; so that it would be deeply sensible that the second stain was worse than the first. It is not a question of returning to God, because a *return* presupposes a departure; and if we are in God, we have but to abide in him; just as, when there arises a little cloud in the middle region of air, if the wind blows, it moves the clouds, but does not dissipate them. If, on the contrary, the sun shines forth, they will soon be dispelled. The more subtle and delicate the clouds are, the more quickly they will be dissipated.

Oh! If we had sufficient fidelity never to look at ourselves, what progress might we not make! Our sights of ourselves resemble certain plants in the sea, which, just so long as their support lasts, prevent bodies from falling. If the branches are very delicate, the weight of the body forces them down, and we are only delayed for a moment; but if we look at ourselves willingly and long, we shall be delayed just so long a time as the look may occupy, and our loss will be great indeed. The defects of this state are certain light emotions or sights of self, which are born and die in a moment—certain winds of self, which pass over the calm sea, and cause ripples; but these faults are taken from us little by little, and continually become more delicate.

The soul, on leaving the tomb, finds itself, without knowing how, clothed with the *inclinations* of Christ; not by distinct and natural views of him, but by its natural condition, finding these inclinations just when they are needed, without thinking of them; as a person who possesses a hidden treasure might find it unexpectedly in the time of his need. The soul is surprised when, without having reflected on the mind and disposition of Christ, it finds them naturally implanted within it. These dispositions of Christ are lowliness, meekness, submission, and the other virtues which he possessed. The soul finds that all these are acting within it, but so easily, that they seem to have become natural to it. Its treasury is in God alone, where it can draw upon it ceaselessly in every time of need, without in any degree diminishing it. It is then that it really "puts on" Jesus Christ (Rom. 13:14); and it is henceforth he who acts, speaks, moves in the soul, the Lord Jesus Christ being its moving principle. Now those around it do not inconvenience it; the heart is enlarged to contain them. It desires neither activity nor retreat, but only to be each moment what God makes it to be.

As in this condition the soul is capable of infinite advancement, I leave those who are living in it to write of it, the light not being given me for the higher degrees, and my soul not being sufficiently advanced in God to see or to know them. All that I shall add is, that it is easy to see by the length of the road necessary to be taken in order to arrive at God that the end is not so soon attained as we are apt to imagine, and that even the most spiritual and enlightened [souls] mistake the consummation of the *passive way of light and love* for the end of this one, when in reality it is but the commencement.

137

I must also remark, that what I have said touching the *mind* of Christ commences as soon as we enter the way of *naked faith*. Although the soul in the former degrees has no distinct sights of Christ, it has nevertheless a desire to be conformed to his image. It covets the cross, lowliness, poverty; then this desire is lost, and there remains a secret inclination for the same things, which continually deepens and simplifies, becoming every day more intimate and more hidden. But here the mind of Christ is the mind of the soul, natural and habitual to it, as something no longer distinct from itself, but as its own being and its own life; Christ exercising it without going out of the soul, and the soul exercising it with him, in him, without going out of him; not like something distinct, which it knows, sees, attempts, practices, but as that which is natural to it. All the actions of life, such as breathing, are done naturally, without thought, rule, or measure; and they are done unconsciously by the person who does them. It is thus with the mind of Christ in this degree, which continually develops, as the soul is more transformed in him, and becomes more thoroughly one with him.

But are there no crosses in this condition? As the soul is strong with the strength of God himself, God lays upon it more crosses and heavier ones than before; but they are borne divinely. Formerly the cross charmed it; it was loved and cherished; now it is not thought of, but is suffered to go and come; and the cross itself becomes God, like all other things. This does not involve the cessation of suffering, but of the sorrow, the anxiety, the bitterness of suffering. It is true that the crosses are no longer crosses, but God. In the former stages, the cross is virtue, and is exalted more and more as the condition is more advanced: here the soul feels it to be God, like the rest; all that constitutes the life of this soul, all that it has, moment by moment, being God to it. The outward appearance of these persons is quite ordinary, and nothing unusual is observed in them except by those who are capable of understanding them.

All is seen in God, and in its true light; therefore this state is not subject to deception. There are no visions, revelations, ecstasies, ravishments, or translations. All these things do not belong to this state, which is above them all. This way is simple, pure, and naked, seeing nothing out of God; and thus seeing all as God sees it, and with his eyes.

Part II

Chapter i

More Particular Description of Several Characteristics of the Resurrection Life

More particular description of some of the characteristics of the divine resurrection life—True liberty and the risen life, in distinction from that which is not so, of which Job is an illustration—Commencement of the apostolic life—Its functions and its fruits—On the practice of virtue, particularly of humility—Blessedness of being lost in God—Rarity of perfect abandonment—Rays of glory escaped from within.

I omitted to say that this is where true liberty begins; not, as some imagine, a liberty which necessitates idleness. That would be imprisonment rather than liberty, fancying ourselves free because, having an aversion to our own works, we no longer practice them. The liberty of which I speak is of a different nature; it does all things easily which God would have done, and the more easily in proportion to the duration and the painfulness of the incapacity to do them which we have previously experienced. I confess I do not understand the resurrection state of certain Christians, who profess to have attained it, and who yet remain all their lives powerless and destitute; for here the soul takes up a true life. The actions of a raised man are the actions of life; and if the soul remain lifeless, I say that it may be dead or buried, but not risen. A risen soul should be able to perform without difficulty all the actions which it has performed in the past, only they would be done in God. Did not Lazarus, after his resurrection, exercise all the functions of life as formerly, and Jesus Christ after his resurrection was willing to eat and to converse with men? And so of those who believe themselves to be risen with Christ, and who are nevertheless stunted in their spiritual growth and incapable of devotion—I say, that they do not possess a resurrection life, for there everything is restored to the soul a hundredfold.

There is a beautiful illustration of this in the case of Job, whose history I consider a mirror of the spiritual life. First God robbed him of his wealth, which we may consider as setting forth gifts and graces; then of his children; this signifies the destruction of natural sensibilities, and of our own works, which are as our children and our most cherished possessions: then God deprived him of his health, which symbolizes the loss of virtue; then he touched his person, rendering him an object of horror and contempt. It even appears that this holy man was guilty of sin, and failed in resignation; he was accused by his friends of being justly punished for his crimes; there was no healthy part left in him. But after he had been brought down to the dunghill, and reduced as it were to a corpse, did not God restore everything to him, his wealth, his children, his health, and his life?

It is the same with spiritual resurrection; everything is restored, with a wonderful power to use it without being defiled by it, clinging to it without appropriating it as before. All is done in God, and things are used as though they were not used. It is here that true liberty and true life are found. "If we have been planted in the likeness of Christ's death, we shall be also in the likeness of his resurrection" (Rom. 6:5). Can there be freedom where there are powerlessness and restrictions? No; "If the Son shall make you free, ye shall be free indeed," but with his liberty.

This is where true liberty begins. Nothing that God desires is difficult to us, or costs us anything; and if a person is called to preach, to instruct, etc., he does it with a marvelous facility, without the necessity of preparing a discourse, being well able to practice what Jesus commanded his disciples,

> Take no thought how or what ye shall speak: for I will give you a mouth and wisdom, which all your adversaries shall not be able to gainsay nor resist. (Matt. 10:19; Luke 21:15)

This is not given till after an experience of powerlessness; and the deeper that experience has been, the greater is the liberty. But it is useless to endeavor to force ourselves into this condition; for as God would not be the source, we should not realize the desired results. It may well be said of this risen life, that all good things are given with it. In this state, the soul cannot practice the virtues as virtues; it is not even conscious of them; but all the virtues have become so habitual to it, that it practices them naturally, almost instinctively.

When it hears others speak of deep humiliation, it is surprised to find that it experiences nothing of the kind; and if it sought to humble itself, it would be astonished, as though it were guilty of unfaithfulness, and would even find it impossible, because the state of annihilation through which it has passed has placed it below all humiliation. For in order to be humbled, we must *be something,* and nothingness cannot be brought lower; its present state has placed it above all humility and all virtue by its transformation into God, so that its powerlessness arises both from its annihilation and its elevation. Those persons have nothing outwardly to distinguish them from others, unless it be that they do no harm to anyone; for, so far as the exterior is concerned, they are very ordinary, and therefore do not attract observation, but live in a state of quiet rest, free from all care and anxiety. They experience a deep joy, arising from the absence of all fear, or desire, or longing, so that nothing can disturb their repose or diminish their joy. David possessed this experience when he said,

> The Lord is my light and my salvation, whom shall I fear? The Lord is the strength of my life; of whom shall I be afraid? (Ps. 27:1)

A heart ravished with joy no longer looks at itself, nor thinks of itself; and its joy, though great, is not an object of contemplation. The soul is in a state of ravishment and ecstasy which cause no uneasiness, because God has enlarged its capacity almost to infinitude. Those ecstasies which cause the loss of consciousness are the effect of human imperfection, and are nevertheless the admiration of men. God is, as it were, drawing the soul out of itself that it may be lost in him; but as it has neither sufficient purity nor strength to bear the process, it becomes necessary, either that God should cease thus to draw it, which involves the cessation of the ecstasy, or that nature should succumb and die, which not infrequently happens. But in this resurrection life, the ecstasy lasts, not for a few hours only, but forever, without either violence or variation, God having purified and strengthened the subject of it to the extent necessary to enable it to bear this glorious ravishment. It seems to me that when God goes out of himself, he creates an ecstasy—but I dare not say this for fear of teaching an error. What I say then is, that the soul drawn out of itself experiences an inward ecstasy; but a happy one, because it is only drawn out of itself in order that it may be drowned and lost in God, quitting its own imperfections and its own limited thoughts to participate in those of God.

O happy nothingness! Where does its blessedness end? O poverty stricken, weary ones! How well ye are recompensed! O unutterable happiness! O soul! What a gain thou hast made in exchange for all thy losses! Couldst thou have believed, when thou wast lying in the dust, that what caused thee so much horror could have procured thee so great a happiness as that which thou now possessest? If it had been told thee, thou couldst not have credited it. Learn now by thine own experience how good it is to trust in God, and that those who put their confidence in him shall never be confounded.

O abandonment! What gladness canst thou impart to the soul, and what progress it might have made if it had found thee at first; from how much weariness it might have been delivered if it had known how to let God work! But, alas! Men are not willing to abandon themselves, and to trust only in God. Even those who appear to do it, and who think themselves well established in it, are only abandoned in imagination, and not in reality. They are willing to abandon themselves in one thing and not in another; they wish to compromise with God, and to place a limit to what they will permit him to do. They want to give themselves up, but on such and such conditions. No; this is not abandonment. An entire and total abandonment excepts nothing, keeps back nothing: neither death, nor life, nor perfection, nor salvation, nor heaven, nor hell. O poor souls! Give yourselves up utterly in this abandonment; you will get only happiness and blessing from it. Walk boldly on this stormy sea, relying on the word of Jesus, who has promised to take upon himself the care of all those who will lose their own life, and abandon themselves to him. But if you sink like Peter, ascribe it to the weakness of your faith. If we had the faith calmly, and without hesitation, to face all dangers, what good should we not receive!

What do you fear, trembling heart? You fear to lose yourself? Alas! For all that you are worth, what would that matter? Yes, you will lose yourself if you have strength to abandon yourself to God, but you will be lost in him. O happy loss! I do not know how sufficiently to repeat it. Why can I not persuade every one to make this abandonment? And why do men preach anything less? Alas! Men are so blind that they regard all this as folly, as something fit for women and weak minds; but for great minds it is too mean; they must guide themselves by their own meager share of wisdom. This path is unknown to them, because they are wise and prudent in themselves; but it is revealed to babes, who can suffer self to be annihilated, and who are willing to be moved by God at his pleasure, leaving him to do with them as he will, without resistance, without considering what others will say.

Oh, how difficult it is to this proper prudence to become nothing both in its own eyes and in the sight of others! Men say that their one object in life is to glorify God, while it is really their own glorification. But to be willing to be nothing in the sight of God, to live in an entire abandonment, in utter self despair, to give themselves to him when they are the most discouraged, to leave themselves in his hands, and not to look at self when they are on the very edge of the abyss; it is this that is so rare, and it is this which constitutes perfect abandonment. There sometimes occur in this life wonderful manifestations to the natural senses, but this is not usual; it is like Christ on the Mount of Transfiguration.

CHAPTER 2

Stability, Experience, Elevation, and Extreme Purity
of the Abandoned Soul

Stability, experiences, elevation, extreme purity, and peace of the soul in the
condition of abandonment—All is purely God to it—For its lost liberty it
finds that of God—State in which all is divinely sure, equal, and indifferent.

The soul having attained a divine state, is, as I have already said, an immovable rock, proof against all blows or shocks, unless it be when the Lord desires it to do something contrary to custom; then, if it does not yield to his first promptings, it has to suffer the pain of a constraint to which it can offer no resistance, and is compelled by a violence which cannot be explained, to obey his will.

It is impossible to tell the strange proofs to which God subjects the hearts which are perfectly abandoned, and which offer no resistance to him in anything; neither, if I could speak of them, should I be understood. All that I can say is, that he does not leave them the shadow of anything that could be named, either in God or out of God. And he so raises them above all by the loss of all, that nothing less than God himself, either in earth or heaven, can stop them. Nothing can harm them, because there is no longer anything hurtful for them, by reason of their union with God, which, in associating with sinners, contracts no defilement, because of its essential purity.

This is more real than I can express: the soul participates in the purity of God. Or rather, all natural purity having been annihilated, the purity of God alone exists in its nothingness. But so truly, that the heart is in perfect ignorance of evil, and powerless to commit it, which does not however prevent the possibility of its falling. But this seldom happens here, because the profound nothingness of the soul does not leave anything that can be appropriated to itself; and it is appropriation alone which can cause sin, for that which no longer exists, cannot sin.

The peace of those in this condition is so invariable and so profound, that nothing either in earth or Hell can disturb it for a moment. The senses are still susceptible to suffering; but when they are overpowered by it, and cry out with the anguish, if they are questioned, or if they examine themselves, they will find nothing in themselves that suffers: in the midst of the greatest pain, they say that they suffer nothing, being unable to admit that they are suffering, because of the divine state of blessedness which reigns in the center or supreme part.

And then there is such an entire and complete separation of the two parts, the inferior and the superior, that they live together like strangers; and the most extraordinary trouble does not interrupt the perfect peace, tranquility, joy, and rest of the superior part; as the joy of the divine life does not prevent the suffering of the inferior.

If you wish to attribute any goodness to those who are thus transformed in God, they will object to it, not being able to find anything in themselves that can be named, affirmed, or heard. They are in a complete *negation*. It is this which causes the difference of terms and expressions employed by writers on this subject, who find a difficulty in making themselves understood, except by those whose experience accords with their own. Another effect of this negation is, that the soul having lost all that was its own, [and] God having substituted himself, it can attribute nothing either to itself or to God; because it knows God only, of whom it can say nothing. Here all is God to the soul, because it is no longer a question of seeing all *in* God; for to see things in God is to distinguish them in him. For instance, if I enter a room, I see all that is there, in addition to the room itself, though it be placed within it; but if all could be transformed into the room itself, or else were taken out of it, I should see nothing but the room alone. All creatures: *celestial, terrestrial,* or *pure intelligences,* disappear and fade away, and there remains only God himself, as he was before the creation. The soul sees only God everywhere; and all is God; not by thought, sight, or light, but by an identity of condition and a consummation of unity, which, rendering it God by participation, without its being able to see itself, prevents it seeing anything anywhere; it can see no created being out of the Uncreated, the only uncreated One being all and in all.

Men would condemn such a state, saying it makes us something less than the meanest insect; and so it does, not by obstinacy and firmness of purpose, but by powerlessness to interfere with ourselves. You may ask one in this condition,

> "Who leads you to do such and such a thing? Is it God who has told you to do it, or has he made known to you his will concerning it?"

He will reply,

> "I know nothing, and I do not think of knowing anything: all is God and his will; and I no longer know what is meant by the will of God, because that will has become natural to me."

> "But, why should you do this rather than that?"

> "I do not know: I let myself be guided by him who draws me."

> "Why so?"

> "He draws me because I, being no longer anything, am carried along with God, and am drawn by him *alone. He* goes hither and thither: *he* acts; and I am but an instrument, which I neither see nor regard. I have no longer a separate interest, because by the loss of myself I have lost all self interest. Neither am I capable of giving any reason for my conduct, for I no longer have a conduct: yet I act infallibly so long as I have no other principle than that of the Infallible One."

147

And this blind abandonment is the permanent condition of the soul of which I speak; because, having become one with God, it can see nothing but God; for having lost all separateness, self-possession, and distinction, it can no longer be abandoning itself, because, in order to abandon ourselves, we must do something, and have the power of disposing of ourselves.

The soul is in this condition: "hidden *with Christ* in God," (Col. 3:3); *mingled* with him, as the river of which we have spoken is mingled with the sea, so that it can be separated no more. It has the ebb and flow of the sea, no longer by choice, will, and liberty, but by nature: the immense sea having absorbed its shallow limited waters, it participates in all the movements of the sea. It is the sea which bears it, and yet it is not borne, since it has lost its own being; and having no other motion than that of the sea, it acts as the sea acts: not because it naturally possesses the same qualities, but because, having lost all its natural qualities, it has no others but those of the sea, without having the power of ever being anything but sea. It is not, as I have said, that it does not so retain its own nature, that, if God so willed it, in a moment it could be separated from the sea; but he does not do this. Neither does it lose the nature of the creature; and God could, if he pleased, cast it off from his divine bosom: but he does not do it, and the creature acts, as it were, divinely.

But it will be said that by this theory I deprive man of his liberty. Not so; he is no longer free except by an excess of liberty, because he has lost freely all created liberty. He participates in the uncreated freedom, which is not contracted, bounded, limited by anything; and the soul's liberty is so great, so broad, that the whole earth appears to it as a speck, to which it is not confined. It is free to do all and to do nothing. There is no state or condition to which it cannot accommodate itself; it can do all things, and yet takes no part in them. O glorious state! Who can describe thee, and what hast thou to fear or to apprehend? O Paul! Thou couldst say, "who shall separate us from the love of Christ?" "I am persuaded," says the great apostle,

> that neither death, nor life, nor angels, nor principalities, nor powers, nor things present, nor things to come, nor height, nor depth, nor any other creature, shall be able to separate us from the love of God, which is in Christ Jesus our Lord. (Rom. 8:35, 38, 39)

Now these words, "I am persuaded," exclude all doubt. But what was the foundation of Paul's assurance? It was in the infallibility of God alone. The epistles of this great apostle, this mystical teacher, are often read, but seldom understood; yet all the mystic way, its commencement, its progress, its end, are described by S. Paul, and even the divine life; but few are able to understand it, and those to whom the light is given see it all there clearer than the day.

Ah! If those who find it so difficult to leave themselves to God could only experience this, they would confess that, though the way might be arduous, a single day of this life was a sufficient recompense for years of trouble. But by what means does God bring the soul here? By ways altogether opposed to natural wisdom and imagination. He builds up by casting down; he gives life by killing. Oh! If I could tell what he does, and the strange means which he uses to bring us here. But silence! Men are not able to hear it; those who have experienced it know what it is. Here there is no need of place or time; all is alike, all places are good; and wherever the order of God may take us, it is well, because all means are useless and infinitely surpassed: when we have reached the end, there is nothing left to wish for.

Here all is God: God is everywhere and in everything, and therefore to the soul all is the same. Its religion is God himself, always the same, never interrupted; and if sometimes God pours some stream of his glory upon its natural powers and sensibilities, it has no effect upon the center, which is always the same. The soul is indifferent either to solitude or a crowd: it no longer looks forward to deliverance from the body in order that it may be united to God. It is now not only united, but transformed, changed into the Object of its love, which causes it no longer to think of loving; for it loves God with his own love, and naturally, though not inamissibly.[1]

---

[1] *Inamissible*: incapable of being lost. Antonym: *amissible*, liable to be lost. (*Webster's Revised Unabridged Dictionary*, 1996, 1998.)

CHAPTER 3

Perfect Union or Deiformity

In which is explained by a comparison, that which concerns perfect union or Deiformity—Secrets of God revealed to his hidden ones, and by them to others—Permanence and progress of this condition, though variable—Natural capacity must be lost—The participated capacity of God by transformation glows infinitely.

A similitude occurs to my mind which appears very appropriate to this subject: it is that of grain. First it is separated from the husk, which sets forth conversion and separation from sin: when the grain is separate and pure, it must be ground (by affliction, crosses, sickness, etc.); when it is thus bruised and reduced to flour, there must still be taken from it, not that which is impure, for this is gone, but all that is coarse, that is, the bran; and when there is nothing left but the fine flour, then it is made into bread for food. It appears as though the flour were soiled, blackened, and blighted; that its delicacy and whiteness were taken from it, in order that it may be made into a paste which is far less beautiful than the flour.

151

Lastly, this paste is exposed to the heat of the fire. Now this is precisely what happens to the soul of which I have been speaking. But after the bread is baked, it is fit for the mouth of the king, who not only unites it to himself by contact with it, but eats it, digests it, consumes it, and annihilates it, that it may enter into his composition, and become part of himself.

You will observe that though the bread has been eaten by the king, which is the greatest honor it can receive, and is its end, yet it cannot be changed into his substance unless it be annihilated by digestion, losing all its natural form and quality. Oh, how well this sets forth all the conditions of the soul; that of union being very different to that of transformation, in which the soul, in order to become one with God, transformed and changed into him, must not only be eaten, but digested, that, after having lost all that was its own, it may become one with God himself:

> That they all may be one, as thou, Father, art in me, and I in thee; that they also may be one in us, I in them, and thou in me, that they may be made perfect in one. (John 17:21, 23)

> He that is joined unto the Lord is one spirit. (I Cor. 6:17)

This state is very little known, therefore it is not spoken of. O state of life! How narrow is the way which leadeth unto thee! O love the most pure of all, because thou art God himself! O love immense and independent, which nothing can limit or straiten!

Yet these people appear quite common, as I have said, because they have nothing outwardly to distinguish them, unless it be an infinite freedom, which is often scandalized by those who are limited and confined within themselves, to whom, as they see nothing better than they have themselves, all that is different to what they possess appears evil. But the holiness of these simple and innocent ones whom they despise is a holiness incomparably more eminent than all which they consider holy, because their own works, though performed with such strictness, have no more strength than the principle in which they originate, which is always the effort, though raised and ennobled, of a weak creature. But those who are consummated in the divine union, act in God by a principle of infinite strength; and thus their smallest actions are more agreeable to God than the multitude of heroic deeds achieved by others, which appear so great in the sight of men. Therefore those in this degree do not seek for great things to do, resting contented with being what God makes them at each moment. These do more, without doing anything, for the conversion of a kingdom, than five hundred preachers who have not attained this condition.

God sometimes, however, permits these people to be known, though not fully. Many people apply to them for instruction, to whom they communicate a vivifying principle, by means of which many more are won to Christ; but this is done, without care or anxiety, by pure Providence. If people only knew the glory which is rendered to God by such as these, who are scorned by the world, they would be astonished; for it is they who render to God a glory worthy of himself; because God, acting as God within them, brings into them a glory worthy of him.

Oh, how many Christians, quite seraphic in appearance, are far from this! But in this condition, as in all others, there are souls more or less divine. God hides them in his bosom, and under the veil of a most common life, so that they may be known to him alone, though they are his delight. Here the secrets of God, in himself and in the hearts of those in whom he dwells, are revealed; not by word, sight, or light, but by the science of God, which abides in him; and when such people have to write or speak, they are themselves astonished to find that all flows from a divine center, without their having been aware that they possessed such treasures. They find themselves in a profound science, without memory or recollection; like an inestimable treasure, which is unobserved until there is a necessity for its manifestation; and it is in the manifestation to others that they find the revelation to themselves. When they write, they are astonished to find themselves writing of things with which they neither knew nor believed themselves to be acquainted; although, as they write, they cannot doubt their apprehension of them. It is not so with other Christians; their light precedes their experience, as a person sees from afar the things which he does not possess, and describes what he has seen, known, heard, etc. But these are persons who hold a treasure within themselves, which they do not see until after the manifestation, although it is in their possession.

Yet, after all, this does not well express the idea which I wish to convey. God is in this soul; or rather the soul no longer exists; it no longer acts, but God acts, and it is the instrument. God includes all treasures in himself, and manifests them through this soul to others; and thus, as it draws them from its center, it becomes aware of their presence, though it had never reflected upon them before. I am sure that any who have attained this degree will enter into my meaning, and will easily distinguish the difference between the states I have described. Those whom I mentioned first, see things and enjoy them as we enjoy the sun; but the others have become one with the sun itself, which does not enjoy nor reflect upon its own light. This condition is permanent, and its only vicissitude [changeableness], so far as its center is concerned, is a greater advancement in God: and as God is infinite, he can continually make the soul more divine by enlarging its capacity, as the water of which we have spoken expands in proportion as it is lost in the sea, with which it mingles incessantly without ever leaving it. It is the same with these souls.

All who are in this degree have God, but some more and some less fully. They are all full, but all do not possess an equal plenitude. A little vase when full is as truly filled as a larger one, yet it does not contain an equal quantity. So all these souls are filled with the fullness of God, but it is according to their receptive capacity, which capacity God continually enlarges. Therefore the longer Christians live in this divine condition, the more they expand, and their capacity becomes continually more immense, without anything being left for them to do or desire; for they always possess God in his fullness, and he never leaves an empty corner in their hearts. As they grow and enlarge, he fills them with himself, as we see with the air. A small room is full of air, but a large one contains more. If you continually increase the size of a room, in the same proportion the air will enter, infallibly though imperceptibly: and thus, without changing its state or disposition, and without any new sensation, the soul increases in capacity and in plenitude. But this growing capacity can only be received in a state of nothingness, because in any other condition there is an opposition to growth.

It may be well here to explain what may appear a contradiction, when I say, that the soul must be brought to nothing in order to pass into God, and that it must lose all that is its own; and yet I speak of capacity which it retains.

There are two capacities. One is natural to the creature, and this is narrow and limited: when it is purified, it is fitted to receive the *gifts of God*, but not God himself; because what we receive within us must of necessity be less than ourselves, as that which is enclosed in a vase must be of less extent, though it may be of greater value, than the vase which contains it.

But the capacity of which I speak here is a capacity to extend and to lose itself more and more in God, after the soul has lost its appropriation, which confined it to itself; and this capacity being no longer restricted nor limited, because its annihilation has deprived it of all form, disposes the soul to flow into God, so that it loses itself, and flows into him who is beyond comprehension. The more it is lost in him, the more it develops and becomes immense, participating in his perfections, and being more and more transformed in him, as water in communication with its source continually mingles with it. God, being our original source, has created us with a nature fit to be united, transformed, and made one with himself.

Chapter 4

Actions and Sufferings of Those in a State of Union with God

The first movements of these souls are divine—Their sufferings are not by reflection, but by impression—Greatness of these sufferings, which, however, do not vary their rest or contentment because of their deification, which progresses infinitely, but gradually—Their peace disturbed neither by good nor evil, as God is neither troubled nor disturbed by the sight of man's sin, all things contributing to his glory.

The soul has now nothing to do but to remain as it is, and to follow without resistance all the movements of its Guide. All its movements are of God, and he guides it infallibly. It is not thus in the inferior conditions, unless it be when the soul begins to taste of the center; but then it is not so infallible, and they would be deceived who applied this rule to any but the most advanced state.

It is the duty of this soul to follow blindly with reflection all the movings of God. Here all reflection is banished, and the soul would find a difficulty in indulging in it, even if it desired to do so. But as by an effort it might accomplish it, this habit should be scrupulously avoided; because reflection alone has the power of leading man to enter into himself, and of drawing him out of God. Now, I say, that if man does not go out of God he will never sin; and if he sin, it is because he has gone out of him, which can only be the effect of appropriation [deliberate acquisition]; and the soul can only take itself back from its abandonment by reflex [returning] action, which would be to it a Hell similar to that into which the great angel fell when, looking with complacency upon himself, and preferring himself to God, he became a devil. And this state would be more terrible as that which had been previously attained was more advanced.

It will be objected that suffering is impossible in this condition, not only as to the center, but also as to the senses, because in order to suffer there must be reflex action, and it is reflection which constitutes the principal and the most painful part of suffering. All this is true in a certain sense; and as it is a fact that souls far less advanced than these suffer sometimes by reflection, sometimes by impression, I maintain that it is also true that those in this degree cannot suffer otherwise than by impression. This does not imply that sorrow may not be unlimited, and far more intense than that which is reflected, as the burning of one brought into actual contact with fire would be much more severe than that of one who is burned by the reflection of fire. It will be said, "But God can teach them by means of reflection how to suffer." God will not make use of reflection for this end. He can show them in a moment what they have to suffer by a direct view, and not by a reflected one, as those in heaven see in God that which is in Him, and that which passes out from Him to his creatures, without looking at these things or reflecting upon them, but remaining absorbed and lost in God. It is this which deceives so many spiritually-minded people, who imagine that nothing can be either known or suffered but by reflection. On the contrary, this kind of knowledge and suffering is very slight compared to that which is imparted in other ways.

All such suffering as can be distinguished and known, though expressed in such exaggerated terms, does not equal that of those who do not know their suffering, and cannot admit that they do suffer, because of the great separation between the two parts. It is true that they suffer extreme pain; it is true that they suffer nothing, and that they are in a state of perfect contentment.

I believe that, if such a soul were taken to Hell, it would suffer all the cruel tortures of its fate in a complete contentment, because of the beatitude of its transformed center; and this is the cause of the indifference which it feels towards all conditions.

As I have said, this does not prevent their [these souls] experiencing the extremity of suffering, as the extremity of suffering does not hinder their perfect happiness. Those who have experienced it will be well able to understand me.

It is not here as in the passive state of love. There the soul is filled with a love of suffering and of the good pleasure of God: here it is a loss of the will in God by a state of deification, where all is God without its being recognized as such. The soul is established by its condition in its sovereign, unchangeable good. It is in a perfect beatitude, where nothing can cross its perfect happiness, which is rendered its permanent condition; for many possess it temporarily, or know it temporarily, before it becomes their permanent condition. God gives first the knowledge of the condition, then a desire for it; then he gives it confusedly and indistinctly; and lastly, he makes it a normal condition, and establishes the soul in it forever.

It will be said that when once the soul is established in this condition, nothing more can be done for it. It is just the reverse: there is always an infinitude to be done on the part of God, not on that of the creature. God does not make the life divine all at once, but by degrees. Then, as I have said, he enlarges the capacity of the soul, and can continually deify it more and more, God being an unfathomable depth.

O Lord! "How great is thy goodness, which thou hast laid up for them that fear Thee!" (Ps. 31:19). It was the sight of this state of blessedness which elicited such frequent exclamations from David after he had been purified from sin.

These persons can no longer be astonished either at any grace that may be given them or at any sin that can be committed, knowing thoroughly both the goodness of God, which causes the one, and the depravity of man, which is the source of the other. Though the whole world might perish, they would not be troubled by it. Is it because they are no longer jealous for the honor of God that they are not troubled by the sin they see around them? No; it is not that: it is that they are jealous for the glory of God *as God*.

God necessarily cares more for his glory than any other can; and all that he does in himself, and out of himself in others, he does for himself. Yet he cannot be troubled by the sins of the world or by the loss of men, although, in order to save them, he became incarnate, and took a mortal body, and gave his life. These Christians also would give a thousand lives to save men; because God, who has transformed them, makes them participate in his qualities, and they see all in the light of God: and although God truly desires the salvation of men, and offers to them all that is necessary for their salvation, though by their own fault it is not efficacious [producing a desired effect] for them, yet he does not fail to promote his glory by their loss; because it is impossible that God should permit anything by which he cannot be glorified, either by justice or by mercy.

This is not the intention of those who offend him, and who render him active dishonor. On the part of God there is no passive dishonor; so it is unavoidable that, even against the will of the sinner, his sin should redound [return, recoil] to the glory of God. Although God's nature cannot be offended, he who sins against Him deserves infinite punishment because of his willingness to offend such infinite goodness; and if he does not professedly oppose God, he yet does so by his actions and his will. And this will is so malicious, that if it could rob God of his divinity, it would do so. It is, then, this malicious will, and not the outward action, which constitutes the offence; for if a person whose will was lost, hidden, and transformed in God were compelled by absolute force to commit sinful actions, it is obvious that he would not sin in committing them.

But in conclusion, say that these persons cannot be troubled by sin, because, although they hate it infinitely, they no longer suffer from it, seeing it as God sees it; and though, if it were necessary, they would give their lives to prevent the commission of a single sin, if God so willed it, they are without action, without desire, without inclination, without choice, without impatience, in a state of complete death, seeing things only as God sees them, and judging them only with God's judgment.

A Short Method of Prayer and Other Writings

The text of this book is set in Goudy Old Style and Goudy Small Caps with Woodtype Ornaments.

Typeset in Corel Ventura Publisher.

Preface of Hendrickson Christian Classics edition by Patricia Klein.

Copyediting, interior design, and production by
Publication Resources, Inc., of Ipswich, MA.
www.pubresources.com